Olivier de Vleeschouwer

Greenhouses and Conservatories

Flammarion

Contents

Foreword

A rusty framework stands out among the tangled under-growth of a forgotten garden, like a ship emerging from a vanished world. As night falls the greenhouse is a favorite meeting-place for blackbirds, but by day, curious children and passing visitors with a taste for adventure can step inside and find themselves transported back in time. Once the visitor's curiosity is aroused, thorny wild roses or stinging nettles are hardly enough to keep him away. The coppery daylilies (*Hemerocallis*) seem to nod assent, their pointed leaves indicating the easi-est way through to the glass and steel house. A fam-ily of ferns, nestling in the shade of three mossy steps, bids a welcome, their outspread fronds like the fingers of a hand. Ferns and greenhouses are old friends: in the nineteenth century, certain col-lectors erected palaces to their beauty. If the visitor paused to admire the ferns at his feet, they would look as lovely as their botanical cousins, the tree ferns. But discretion is part of their charm, and the eager visitor brushes past, intent on his goal, through the creaking door into the silence of this sanctuary. There is no one in the greenhouse, yet it is full of life. The gardener has gone, but each pot bears his fingerprints, and the whole greenhouse seems to be in a state of suspended animation, awaiting his return. The greenhouse is a refuge, a world apart, as silent as a country church, while the air seems full of secrets.

The atmosphere of the place holds the humbled visitor in its grip. Life itself is at stake here, where nature works its magic in splendor and sim-plicity. The greenhouse grants man the inordinate powers of a deity: it is he who proveides earth, water, heat, and light. Seeds germinate, cuttings take root, and though these processes may have a rational explana-tion, they retain an element of mystery, the mystery of the seed that sprouts while it is still cold outside, the fruit that ripens before its time, the flower that blooms out of season. The signs of the miracle-worker's ritual and all the paraphernalia of the gardener's art are everywhere in the deserted greenhouse: earth mixed with sand, sieves, dented old watering-cans, buckets of peat, wooden boxes, faded labels.

If you were to close your eyes and use your sense of smell, amother range of sensations emerges: the greenhouse is host to a whole range of rich, warm, damp, and earthy scents. Is this one peppermint or African marigold? Is this a scarlet pelargonium or a tomato leaf crushed between the fingers? Don't be

Page 1: The glass roof of a conservatory reflected in a mirror.
Page 2: The hot, humid atmosphere of a greenhouse for tropical plants. The Preston Park conservatory was designed by the British firm Amdega (pages 4 and 5).
In this magnificent greenhouse from the early 1900s, cast iron and palm leaves interact in a play of light and shade (facing page).
The glass roof protects the plants in this old French greenhouse, but attracts birds (above).

surprised if scents like these spring from the pages of this book, like a tender tribute to a garden you once knew. The memory lane of childhood is full of sights, sounds, and smells, which keep the beauties of the past alive.

The light is beginning to fade, but it's hard to leave this special place. Beneath its lovely transparent shell, the greenhouse not only protects plants; it is also a place where dreams come true, where the future looks bright and full of promise. The greenhouse's single aim is to keep its occupants happy and thriving: witness the lizard that comes in to cool down under the gurgling tap. And when the gardener comes back, as he surely will, he will pick up his work where he left off, with the modesty and confidence of one who knows that the seed will become a flower. Such modesty is a gift, but it is cultivated only through art.

Nature no longer needs a gardener in the fall, as illustrated here in the greenhouses of Saint-Jean-de-Beauregard, near Paris (previous double page and above). When vines are cultivated under glass, grapes can be served at Christmas. Elsewhere, luxuriant vegetation holds sway: this conservatory is part of a private house in Nîmes, southern France (facing page).

From the Orangery to the Conservatory

Gardeners in both ancient China and the Roman Empire used to protect certain tender plants during the cold season. The concept of the modern greenhouse, however, originated in the mobile constructions that were devised during the Renaissance to shelter new plant species brought back from the Hispanic or British colonial empires.

A shelter for new plants

The great maritime expeditions of the Renaissance divided the world into colonial empires; as a result, trade expanded rapidly from the middle of the fifteenth century onward. Exotic fruits from Africa, America, or Asia were introduced into Europe. Princes and wealthy merchants were keen to impress their peers by acquiring hitherto unknown species. Botanic gardens had recently been created to cultivate medicinal plants and to teach medical students about the sources of most of the remedies they used; the collections in these gardens were considerably enriched with the seeds, bulbs, and young plants that navigators brought back from their voyages. Amateur botanists were also fascinated by these discoveries, but a major problem soon arose: how to conserve fashionable species such as citrus fruit, myrtles, oleanders, and pomegranate trees, which were totally unaccustomed to the harsh climate of northern Europe. A collector with only a few orange trees in tubs could always find a place to shelter them during the cold season. And when these citrus trees were planted in the open ground, it was still

quite easy to enclose them with protective shutters. In the sixteenth century, wooden or stone structures were built to protect certain fruit trees, such as the delicate Seville orange. These "winter shelters" were sometimes heated by candles, or by small fires that had to be watched regularly.

Larger collections of citrus fruit, however, required other methods, and the courts at Munich, Stuttgart, or Heidelberg were the first to experiment. Orange trees were planted in rows in the open ground, and as soon as the cold weather arrived, a mobile construction was set up to protect them. This consisted of a sort of framework on wheels, partly covered with wooden boards to shelter the plants from the elements. Detachable panels let light and air through as necessary. The Heidelberg model, designed for the Elector Palatine, as the local prince was called, was 262 feet (80 meters) long and sheltered no fewer than 400 trees. This solution, though ingenious, had several disadvantages: it provided less than adequate insulation, its joints

In the Versailles orangery, orange and lemon trees are sheltered from the cold during the winter months (page 12). The amateur gardener can now create a "Versailles" touch: the sturdy but decorative wooden tubs made in the eighteenth century for Versailles are now copied and made available for everyone. Like all other orangeries, this one at Castle Ashby in Northamptonshire was built so that tender plants could survive the harsh north European climate (facing page). These fragrant, floral places (above: *The Royal Pavilion*, by Humphry Repton, 1808) gradually became architectural masterpieces of elegance and refinement. The spectacular Alton Towers conservatory in Staffordshire is a striking example (following double page).

were damaged by repeated dismantling operations, and it was expensive.

To overcome these difficulties, the structure was given more fixed parts and fewer movable ones. The north-facing wall and the two side walls became permanent, so that only the roof and the south wall needed covering over in the winter. Before long, the roof also became a permanent element in the structure. The midday sun shone in through tall, small-paned windows to warm the plants inside. These first "orangeries," built in stone, brick, or wood, appeared in the Netherlands. The original, strictly utilitarian shelters gradually became more attractive buildings, no doubt because they were designed to suit their palatial surroundings.

Nevertheless, these early orangeries were of simple design and relatively modest dimensions. Since their initial purpose was to provide an environment in which plants would be protected from frost, rudimentary heating systems were gradually installed. Wood-burning earthenware stoves or iron stoves fed with peat were the most common heating methods. Orangeries were at first almost exclusively reserved for orange trees (from the late fifteenth century on, the orange was the favorite among citrus fruits and

considered a sign of prestige in high society), but they gradually became home to myrtles and lemon or pomegranate trees, then to a host of plants that had previously been of interest only to botanic gardens.

The first of these gardens were established in Pisa and Padua in 1543; many others sprang up throughout Europe in the years that followed. The Leipzig garden, for example, dates from 1580, and the Leiden garden from 1587. Their botanists had a major task to accomplish: defining and cataloging a multitude of new imported species. The gardens were also centers for research and exchange, thanks to which the fortunate few, who had so far been chiefly interested in citrus fruits, learned of the existence of these new species. Orangeries needed a new name, now that orange trees were not the only

At first, the orangery was a rudimentary structure, situated some distance from the house; it was soon moved closer, however, and eventually became a model of courtly elegance. This anonymous drawing of a model with thirteen windows (above), and the orangery in Kensington Gardens in London (facing page), testify to this evolution. These vast buildings were designed to house citrus fruit trees (highly fashionable at the time) and to serve as a setting for all kinds of festivities.

species grown in them. They became known as "greenhouses," which housed all manner of plants, not only the tender evergreens that gave them their English name.

Meanwhile, a new trend was emerging: during the summer months, when the plants were taken out, human beings moved in. The greenhouse became a setting for social gatherings. This practice eventually proved extremely popular; indeed, the word "greenhouse" now conjures up pictures of Victorian conservatories, where family and friends sipped their tea among the ferns and daturas. In the seventeenth century, however, the greenhouse was still the prerogative of royalty: it provided an original décor for their festivities, which became less formal away from the constraints of court.

As attitudes changed, so did heating methods. In botanic gardens (especially in the Netherlands and England), architects found ways to replace the old peat- or wood-burning stoves, which sometimes had disastrous effects on the plants by exposing them to too much direct heat. Small rooms in which a single fire was kept alight were often built against north-facing walls. The heat from this fire was circulated throughout the greenhouse via an elaborate network of pipes. Another method (used in the Chelsea Physic Garden in London, for example) was to put the stoves (fed with bark or manure) in the basement, where they heated the greenhouse just as efficiently but took up less room. Double walls were sometimes built, with straw stuffed between them to provide more efficient insulation. Elsewhere, the temperature was regulated by stuffing straw between the ceiling and the roof, or by placing wooden shutters or curtains at the greenhouse windows. In the 1760s, Diderot and D'Alembert's *Encyclopedia*, an attempt to codify and comprehend the natural world typical of the Enlightenment, included descriptions of such greenhouses, with many annotations. Diderot particularly mentions the lead taken by the Dutch in this field. A Dutch naturalist, Dr. Hermann Boerhaave (director of the Leiden Botanic Garden from 1709 to 1730), studied the best way of using the sun's rays to ensure heat and light inside the buildings. He invented the use of sliding glass panels, which allowed the low winter sun to shine into the greenhouse vertically, whereas in summer its rays formed an angle of 45 degrees with the roof. This method, which reduced the sun's harmful effect on certain plants, was used nearly a hundred years later by John Claudius Loudon (1783–1843), a Scot with a passion for gardens and greenhouses, who was convinced that a curved, slanting roof was essential to the successful cultivation of many plant species.

Botanic gardens played a vital role in reseach into the production and conservation of plants. Their collections drew huge crowds of admiring visitors, who were curious to see the new flowers and foliage that explorers had brought back from their expeditions.
Above, the newly constructed temperate greenhouse in the Jardin des Plantes, Paris (watercolor by Victor-Jean Nicolle, 1810). Among the luxuriant vegetation of Provence, the Mas des Arnajons orangery looks temptingly refreshing (facing page); it also protects plants during cold winters.

Baroque orangeries

At Heidelberg, the garden of the Elector Palatine boasted an ingenious orangery, which could be dismantled. It was designed in 1620 by the architect Salomon de Caus, who also drew up plans for an orangery with permanent walls on the sides and the north aspect. A century later, the one at the twin palaces of the Belvedere in Vienna was built on this model.

The Belvedere marks a definite break with the makeshift, strictly utilitarian orangeries of the past. The first difference was the geographical position of the orangery, which adjoined one of the palaces itself rather than being constructed some distance away. Over the years the orangery, then the greenhouse, moved nearer and nearer to the house itself, until the indoor garden became an integral part of its architecture. This proximity meant that aesthetic changes were also made. The three permanent walls of the Belvedere orangery were therefore imposing and richly ornamented. They were built to last and to be admired; they were the setting for French doors in

the façade, and they supported the roof, consisting of detachable panels the width of a ladder, which could be partially or completely removed. In the early eighteenth century, as the fashion for orangeries spread throughout Europe, these detachable elements became less common. The orangery became a building in its own right, worthy of its noble environment. Moreover, whereas orange trees had formerly been planted in open ground, now they were usually planted in tubs which could easily be taken out in the spring. This meant that the orangery was increasingly used for other purposes, especially for social gatherings of all kinds during fine weather.

In such a charming environment, these events were so pleasant that no self-respecting court wished to be outdone. Architects vied with each other to satisfy the desires of royalty. French orangeries (at Versailles, for example) were often to be found in various parts of the gardens, whereas German ones were placed next to their owners' houses, and designed to be in perfect harmony with their surroundings. In this baroque age, it was no longer necessary to possess an impressive collection of orange trees in order to have an orangery. What mattered most

The baroque orangeries that flourished in the early eighteenth century corresponded to a thirst for the exotic. At Sezincote House in Gloucestershire, this Indian garden with its octagonal pavilion seems to be straight out of the tales of *A Thousand and One Nights* (facing page). Above, a nineteenth-century English painting of the huge conservatory at Ilford House in Essex.

was what the building symbolized: a certain quality of life at court, for which the orangery provided an ideal setting. Banquets and festivities of all kinds were held there, and the orange trees in their tubs became mere parts of the décor, moved around to suit the occasion. Few people remembered that they were the original *raison d'être* of these stone, brick, and glass buildings.

Orangeries were fashionable in almost all of northern Europe through the mid-eighteenth century. Once the enthusiasm for citrus fruits had waned, however, fewer were built; another reason was that the fashion in gardens had changed. By the late eighteenth century, picturesque gardens had supplanted the orangeries. In Paris, the Jardin du Roi (precursor of the Jardin des Plantes), created by Guy de La Brosse in 1636, was a place

where the public could learn about botany by observing medicinal plants or collections of rare species. The garden was transformed to accommodate the new fashion: for example, a maze consisting of spiral paths led to a little Chinese pavilion, and hothouses were constructed for a large number of exotic plants. These and other changes were signs of the desire for less formal, more romantic landscapes, in which the orangery now looked out of place and out of date.

The Versailles orangery, a huge arched gallery and its supporting structure, painted here by Pierre-Denis Martin (facing page). It once housed 3,000 tender plant species and is still a delightful place to visit. The Orangery in Kensington Gardens (left), a stone's throw from the famous Kensington Palace, makes another charming outing, and includes an elegant tea room. The orangery at the splendid Boboli Gardens in Florence is a secret place, however, where the trees that will adorn the park in summer are sheltered in tightly packed rows (above).

The vogue for greenhouses

During the Age of Enlightenment, passions were aroused by the flood of new knowledge on all manner of subjects, including botany, and expeditions were encouraged. Starting in 1732, essays by great naturalists like Georges-Louis Buffon and Carl Linnaeus furthered the climate of intellectual curiosity that was so propitious for these voyages, which resulted in the discovery of quantities of unknown plant species. Explorers and adventurers also played their part: countless French, Dutch, and British expeditions returned with a wealth of new treasures in the holds of their ships, including rubber and valuable spices. Unfortunately, these voyages sometimes lasted several years,

and their precious collections did not always arrive in perfect condition. In 1833, to overcome this major problem, Dr. Nathaniel Ward, a London physician and botanist, invented a miniature greenhouse which revolutionized the transport of tender species. Before this date, only one plant in twenty survived the voyage. Ward's case reversed the trend: only one plant died for nineteen that survived and were eventually planted out under cover.

While orangeries were becoming common features in Europe's royal or noble houses, private individuals continued to seek better ways of cultivating sheltered plants for domestic use. Botanists and gardeners experimented with slanting frames placed on low walls. In 1730, the Dutch and English took their inspiration from this model to produce the first "hothouse," describe in Diderot and d'Alembert's *Encyclopedia* in 1765. These hothouses, heated by coal-burning stoves, were designed for maximum heat and humidity. They were narrower than the classical orangeries, with a large surface area of glass that enabled them to produce a variety of fruit and vegetables as efficiently as was possible at the time. The problem of using all the light was not seriously faced until the end of the eighteenth century, but some specialists already understood its importance and were looking for the best way to ensure that sheltered plants obtained the light essential for their growth. The fixed structures were obviously too heavy, and glazed wooden frames were found to be an efficient solution, especially as wood and glass could be associated to the best possible effect and at a relatively reasonable price. These

Long before the great greenhouses of the nineteenth and twentieth centuries were constructed, the Malmaison hothouse (near Paris) proved that it was possible to use glass over a very large surface. A smaller building adjoining this one housed the salons, where visitors came to admire the Empress Josephine's famous collections. The invention of miniature greenhouses in the early nineteenth century enabled explorers to bring tender plants back from all over the world. These little wood, glass, and wire mesh shelters (facing page, an 1821 model) re-created the conditions of heat and humidity found in the plants' natural habitat (facing page, top: engraving by A. Thouin).

famous "hothouses," where the temperature exceeded 70°F (21°C), were gradually installed in botanic gardens. They also prompted wealthy amateur botanists to begin collecting rare plant species. None of their collections, however, could have equaled those of Josephine de Beauharnais, wife of the Emperor Napoleon, some sixty years later, at her estate of Malmaison, near Paris. Historians have concentrated on the Empress's taste for clothes and jewelry, but her passion for flowers was such that she commissioned (from the architects Thibaut and Vignon) a sumptuous greenhouse some 164 feet (50 meters) long and 21 feet (6.50 meters) wide, heated by a dozen large coal-burning stoves. It cost about half as much as the purchase price of Malmaison itself, and was even more beautiful than the greenhouse in the Jardin des Plantes in Paris. Visitors could admire Josephine's splendid collections of plants in the comfort of the rooms added at the back of the greenhouse. Malmaison soon boasted one of Europe's largest plant collections, thanks to expert head gardeners such as Delahaye in 1805, who brought back quantities of seeds from Australia;

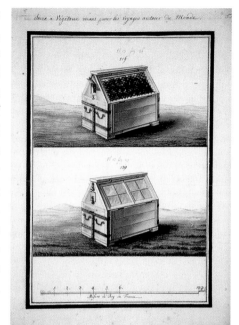

he was replaced by Aimé Bonpland, the botanist on the great explorer Alexander von Humboldt's expedition to Latin America. A contemporary journal reported that Josephine's greenhouse had "184 different species, unknown to the Jardin des Plantes." The Empress was a true enthusiast: she readily invited botanists into her greenhouse and willingly shared her discoveries with herbalists and horticulturists, many of whom were given a variety of seeds and cuttings to take away. Josephine's splendid collection was immortalized by the painter Pierre-Joseph Redouté. After her death in 1824, it was dispersed and the greenhouse was dismantled.

In the early nineteenth century, the pineapple became as fashionable as the orange had once been. Baron Münchhausen (a genuine baron, who had nothing to do with his famous literary namesake) was the proud owner of a pineapple shelter, consisting entirely of glass panels, in which the fruit was grown successfully for the first time in Germany. In France, the novelist Honoré de Balzac was also fascinated by this exotic fruit. In 1837 he bought a garden (18,300 square feet or 1,700 square meters) in Sèvres, south of Paris, where he intended to plant one hundred thousand pineapples. A hothouse was constructed, in which the temperature reached the 68 to 86°F (20 to 30°C) necessary for these plants to bear fruit.

The exotic and mysterious interior of the Malmaison greenhouse inspired this famous watercolor, by Garneray (following double page).

The golden age of botanic gardens

Orangeries were built all over northern Europe, but when it came to greenhouses, England took the lead. The English were traditionally keen gardeners, but more important, their Industrial Revolution began long before that of other countries. England was the first to experience the radical changes that were to affect European countries one by one during the nineteenth century: country-dwellers moved to the cities, the railways expanded at a phenomenal rate, and there were unprecedented social and economic developments. Architects working on the great aristocratic estates put the latest technological and industrial innovations to good use. These domains created the fashion for home-grown exotic plants, and their greenhouses were often costly, impressive buildings.

In his pineapple greenhouse, the famous Baron Münchhausen had already attempted a design in which the surface area of glass was as large as possible, with the light-blocking structural elements reduced to a minimum. Industrial progress now made

such designs easier to produce. When orangeries were in fashion, wood was preferred to stone or brick, because it was less heavy, easier to use, and made it possible to create a light interior. Wood continued to be used in the construction of many greenhouses (although its advantages and disadvantages were debated throughout the nineteenth century), but it was gradually replaced by cast iron. This material opened up new horizons. Apart from the fact that it was frost-resistant and waterproof, it also gave architects the freedom to include vaults, domes, and all manner of fanciful elements in their designs. The possibility of pre-molding elements of the structure made cast iron more attractive than wrought iron, which entailed more archaic methods and was more expensive. Meanwhile, it had become technically possible to produce sheets of glass up to 6 feet (1.80 meters) long, three times longer than in the past. Such progress made a considerable difference, but tender plants from across the world would still not have survived if heating systems had not also undergone significant improvements. Boilers were placed outside the greenhouses, and hot water flowed through an ingenious network of pipes, ensuring a constant temperature throughout the buildings.

The rigid lines of the Great Conservatory in Rouen's Jardin des Plantes (above) give no clue to the exuberance that reigns within. These cacti know nothing of the mists of Normandy, sheltered under glass in the arid atmosphere that suits them well (facing page).

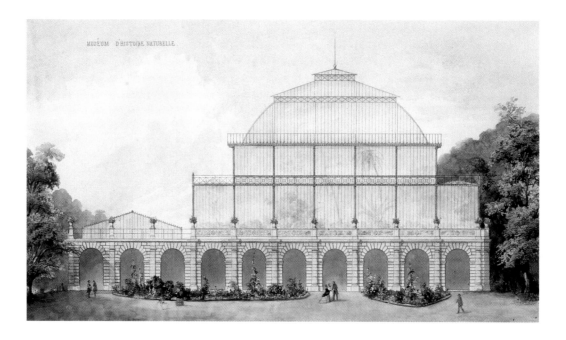

These improvements came about just as wealthy amateur botanists, bored with citrus fruit, were turning their attention to the new species described by renowned botanists. They were able to buy these treasures from nurseries supplied by plant-hunters, who were sometimes as reckless as they were daring. A craze developed for tropical and subtropical plants, with a preference for palm trees of all kinds, which were endlessly fascinating in their infinite variety.

In the nineteenth century, the British Empire covered a quarter of the world's surface; the British were therefore keen to gather as much information as they could about the commercial potential of bananas, cocoa beans, rubber, and cotton. The colonial era was the golden age of botanic gardens, which were no longer exclusively devoted to the cultivation of medicinal plants. The Royal Botanic Gardens, Kew, established in the 1770s by the amalgamation of two neighboring royal gardens (later famous for its Palm House and still a favorite destination for today's Londoners), financed expeditions all over the world and was renowned for its impressive collections. The 1789 printed catalogue already listed as many as 5,500 exotic plants.

Botanists were quick to realize that the orangeries of the past were no longer suited to the great diversity of plants being introduced to Europe. At first, however, most of them thought that all these species needed a temperature above 70°F (21°C) in order to thrive, but this temperature, obtained with coal-burning stoves, turned out to be unsuitable to acclimatize a good many of these unknown species. The hothouses in botanic gardens therefore became increasingly elaborate over the

At the instigation of Adolphe Thiers, then Minister of Public Works, the architect Charles Rohault de Fleury (1801–1875) was assigned to the construction of greenhouses for the Natural History Museum (that is, the Jardin des Plantes) in Paris in 1833. The use of glass over such a large surface was a considerable technological feat at the time.

years, as great efforts were made to reproduce the climate of the natural habitats of these imported species. Botanists defined each plant's needs for humidity, heat, and light. Starting in the early nineteenth century, this differentiation meant that hothouses were divided into two separate areas: one dry and one humid. In the latter (where the temperature was between 77 and 86°F or 25 to 30°C), water tanks, watering systems, and frequent spraying created sufficient humidity to protect certain species which would otherwise have died. Among these, the preference was for orchids: these parasitic plants from Central America became extraordinarily popular, and European collectors bought certain rare varieties at astronomical prices.

The other part of these hothouses was the temperate area, where the temperature was never above 59°F (15°C) nor below 41°F (5°C), and which housed subtropical species such as crotons, caladiums, and dracaenas. In their constant concern to respect each plant's natural habitat, botanists eventually developed cold greenhouses too, where the temperature varied between 37 and 50°F (3 and 10°C): these buildings were often partly constructed in stone, and were therefore reminiscent of the orangeries of the past.

Like the small Victorian girl in Thomas Greenhalgh's painting, today's children still marvel to see the magnificent greenhouses in Kew Gardens.

Follies in glass and steel

As industry advanced and techniques were perfected, greenhouses acquired a growing number of admirers impressed by the horticultural miracles that were inconceivable only a few decades before: the domestication of nature, the taming of whole landscapes beneath the magical transparency of glass.

Despite considerable progress in the late eighteenth century and the early years of the nineteenth, the working of miracles was still very much a matter of chance, and it was extremely difficult to achieve the delicate balance between heat, light, and air. Many plants still died from too much heat or poor ventilation, many species still withered under the mangifying-glass effect of the sun on poor-quality glass, and still others lost their color in the shade. Collectors, who had sometimes spent fortunes on the construction of real follies in glass and steel, saw their hopes dashed: Mother Nature was not yet under their control, and she continued to spring some disastrous surprises.

The main reason for these problems, however, was glass. For a long time in England, it was produced in very thin sheets for economic reasons,

and could only be used in small panes. The first greenhouses were therefore built with overlapping panes, placed on very heavy frameworks which blocked out the light. Moreover, the panes were not watertight where they overlapped. Water got in to the greenhouses, and in winter the frost caused serious damage. The solution to these problems arrived in two stages. First of all, in 1833 a method of mass-producing sheet glass was discovered. This method reduced the number of blowholes and other imperfections that transformed the sun's rays into veritable blowtorches, causing irreparable burns on foliage. Second, in 1845 the tax on glass was abolished. Much larger sheets could now be produced at a reasonable price; consequently, private and public greenhouses were built at a furious pace. Yet these larger-sized sheeets of glass still could not prevent certain plants from drying up. Colored glass was used in the Palm House at Kew Gardens, as it was thought to weaken the sun's rays. This method proved unsatisfactory, however, and the plants were no healthier. The problem was not solved until glass was produced in sheets that were rolled out flat. Before this improvement, the sheets were not uniform in

Built in 1893, the greenhouses at the Jardin des Plantes in Nantes, France, house some superb collections, including 100 bromeliads, wonderful palm trees, and over 4,000 cacti (facing page). In the light of the setting sun, the glass of the Cacti Greenhouse at the Jardin des Plantes in Paris glows pink (above). This phenomenon can be observed in many monumental greenhouses, like that of Laeken in Belgium.

thickness, and they contained imperfections that concentrated the light at fixed points, damaging the health of the plants being cultivated.

As for the framework itself, cast iron had gradually replaced wood in the larger buildings, but wrought iron was still in use. Cast iron was very resistant to pressure, but wrought iron was significantly less sensitive to lateral traction. It could also be used to make thinner bars and to create decorative curves, all of which let more light into the greenhouse. The association of cast iron (for pillars and columns) and wrought iron (for uprights and window bars) made it possible to construct many of the great greenhouses of the day.

This technical progress gave architects greater freedom when designing greenhouses, and accordingly, a number of architectural trends developed. Those who favored greenhouses with rectilinear frames were increasingly challenged by those who preferred the curvilinear model. In 1820, the Duke of Northumberland commissioned Charles Fowler to build the Great Conservatory at Syon Park (near Kew). The duke wanted to house his magnificent collection of plants in a building worthy of their exotic beauty—and Fowler's design, which was indeed original, was considered (by Fowler himself and by many specialists) to be a perfect example of what plants needed. The greenhouse was completed in 1827, and today's visitors can see that it is a perfect synthesis of the baroque orangery and the buildings of its time. Many admirers described its curvilinear structure—280 feet (85 meters) long—as an ideal model for the preservation of tender species. Its glass dome was no doubt

In 1580, Vespasien Robin constructed a small experimental enclosure near the Seine, intended for the cultivation of medicinal plants. Two centuries later, it became the Jardin des Plantes of the Natural History Museum (facing page). Almost every large city in the western world followed the fashion for creating botanic gardens, such as those of Buenos Aires (above).

inspired by Loudon's reflections on the importance of light. Loudon himself, together with other botanist-architects, acknowledged the many qualities of this kind of construction, but they were convinced that it would not suit all plant species.

France was also in the forefront of this architectural adventure. Charles Rohault de Fleury had just been appointed architect of the Jardin des Plantes (previously the Jardin du Roi) when Adolphe Thiers (then Minister of Public Works) decided that Paris needed a much bigger greenhouse than those already in existence, in which the garden's splendid plant collections could be displayed to the best advantage. In 1834, with the help of Neumann,

The Great Conservatory in the botanic garden in Adelaide, Australia, is no doubt one of the world's most spectacularly beautiful (previous double page). It is decorated with a frieze of small blue triangles, which add to the sparkle of the glass architecture, which is as elegant as the surrounding vegetation. The greenhouse at Bicton Gardens (near Exeter in Devon) houses amazing collections of geraniums and fuchsias, as well as plants from temperate and tropical climates. Above, the wrought-iron Palm House, the northern side of which rests against a stone wall.

the head gardener of the Paris Natural History Museum (which includes the Jardin des Plantes), Rohault perfected "the first building consisting simply of an iron frame with glass surfaces." He opted for a rounded roof, with a series of greenhouses which would enjoy maximum sunlight. There were two rectilinear buildings, separated by an esplanade and extended to left and right by glass galleries. Rohault took advantage of the superiority of French glass factories, which could now produce panes measuring 11 3/4 inches by 7 3/4 inches (30 cm by 20 cm); this was a real achievement at the time. Even though the galleries on the right were never built, the greenhouses at the Jardin des Plantes had an impact on public opinion that we can hardly imagine today. Many visitors to the greenhouse still had no glass in their own windows, and most of them had poor-quality heating. Suddenly, they found themselves surrounded by glass in an atmosphere of tropical heat. No doubt their delight was not exclusively due to the exquisite plants on show.

Charles Rohault de Fleury's monumental design for the hothouses in the Paris Jardin des Plantes (above); when they were built in 1834, public acclaim was immediate (left).

Conservatories: from the parlor to the palace

The greenhouse initially replaced the orangery as a place to store or simply to shelter plants. Gradually, however, fashionable society began to seek out these sheltered places where rare plants could be admired. A distinction came about between the greenhouse itself

and the "conservatory," a place devoted to the conservation of plants, but also to leisure and relaxation. The conservatory was usually attached to the house (the winter garden being a larger-scale adaptation of it). The Victorians were very fond of conservatories, which they considered ideal settings for a new lifestyle, but a certain something was still missing. Before long, however, some creative designers set to work to transform the latest industrial progress into a lovely aesthetic effect.

There had been a heated debate over the merits of rectilinear and curvilinear greenhouses. In the private domain, the first great greenhouse constructed with a curvilinear frame was the work of the architect (and gardener) Joseph Paxton (1801–1865), who later designed the famous

Crystal Palace (built in Hyde Park in London for the 1851 Universal Exhibition). The Great Conservatory of Chatsworth was shaped like a clover-leaf. It was commissioned by the Duke of Devonshire, and built by Paxton and Decimus Burton between 1836 and 1840. Apart from its size, it stood out from previous work by its unique use of glass, which covered the entire volume of the building. This construction was illustrated in many contemporary specialist journals, and it had a considerable impact on people's attitudes. Until then, only conservatories attached to houses had achieved such successful transparency, but thanks to their modest dimensions, they could house only a limited number of plants. Chatsworth ushered in a new age, a period of vast buildings enclosing realistic jungles where people could come, alone or with friends, to find calm, tranquility, and a total change of scenery. To this day, although the Conservatory is no longer standing, the great gardens of Chatsworth (in Derbyshire) still draw admiring crowds.

After Paxton's achievement, many enthusiasts wrote articles praising these truly spectacular

From the mid-nineteenth century, every wealthy home acquired a conservatory, which became the favorite place for family gatherings or lovers' trysts. This new, more informal area was perfect for relaxing or sharing secrets. The painting above is the work of Louise Abbema, who also immortalized Sarah Bernhardt's conservatory, where the great tragic actress liked to read in peace and quiet, away from the bustle of the reception rooms.

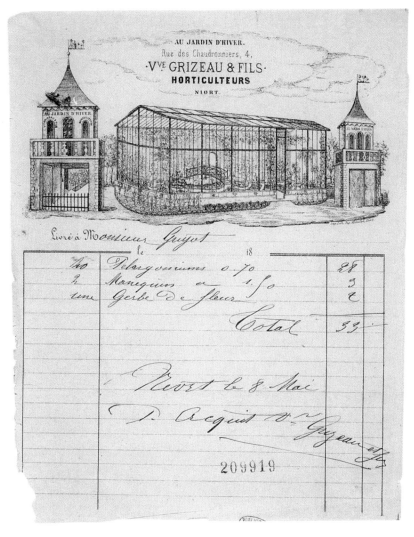

This plan for a conservatory with enameled windows in Clermont-Ferrand, France (above), and the illustration on this nurseryman's bill (left) are proof, if any were needed, of the nineteenth-century passion for greenhouses. The conservatory, with its profusion of plants and Victorian furniture, inspired many a nineteenth-century painter. It was an ideal setting for the genre scenes which were so popular at the time (*The Rivals*, James Tissot, 1875, following double page).

greenhouses. Once the construction techniques had been mastered, all kinds of extravagances became possible. According to Loudon, anyone who wanted to design an imaginative greenhouse was no longer restricted by technical difficulties. Once the practical details were taken care of, people could, for example, stroll along in the shade of the tallest oriental trees and delight in the chirping of a flock of birds from all over the world—or pause by an ornamental lake to enjoy the sight of exotic fish gliding peacefully among the coral (salt water was no problem either).

Many of these flights of fancy were inspired by the first flush of enthusiasm after the construction of the Great Conservatory at Chatsworth, but Paxton's and Loudon's ideas appealed to

Who can tell what this elegant lady is thinking? The model for this 1879 painting by Edouard Manet (*In the Greenhouse*) was an American friend of the artist, famous for her beauty. This work, the first of Manet's paintings bought by a museum, was rediscovered by American soldiers in 1945, hidden at the bottom of a salt mine.

mid-nineteenth-century society, which was fascinated by all things exotic. Starting in 1850, the conservatory created a sensation among middle- and upper-class families. The Industrial Revolution not only furthered technical progress; it also allowed many private individuals to achieve their architectural dreams.

The conservatory was attached to the house, and its roof was always made of glass. During the cold season, the temperature varied between 45 and 54°F (7 and 12°C), but it increased rapidly when the warm weather arrived. It was intended as a place for displaying, rather than cultivating, newly discovered tropical plants. It was also used as a reception room, and was generally an extension of the living room, distinguished from the latter by its glass and steel structure, as well as by its furniture, which was imported from the Orient or copied from Indian, North African, or Far Eastern designs. Bamboo or wrought iron was used to make armchairs, chairs, or tables, on which pots or dishes with Chinese motifs added a final touch of

exoticism. This extraordinary setting was considered ideal for playing cards, reading, or chatting. The conservatory provided a perfect backdrop for amorous meetings: "love among the tree ferns" was a favorite theme for many a great painter (Manet painted *In the Greenhouse* in 1879) or writer. Edith Wharton, for example, herself owner of a fine greenhouse, recently restored, wrote in her great novel *The Age of Innocence* of "the depths of a conservatory where camellias and tree-ferns arched their costly foliage over seats of black and gold bamboo." F. Scott Fitzgerald's *This Side of Paradise* makes the reputation of the conservatory as a place for flirts perfectly clear: "Don't disappear with young men...I don't like finding you in some corner of the conservatory exchanging silliness with any one—or listening to it."

The bourgeoisie thought it a fine idea to teach children about rare plants by taking them to greenhouses. Flowers came in and out of fashion, and in 1890, when Charles Courtney Curran painted *Chrysanthemums* (left), the chrysanthemum had not yet acquired its rather gloomy reputation as a cemetery flower.

Traveling in the comfort of the home: the Orient in the greenhouse

For the famous, the wealthy, the royal, the fashionable, the artistic, and the green-fingered, the conservatory was a privileged place where time stood still, away from the bustle of the outside world—a place where one could become a child again.

Architects interpreted their clients' wildest dreams. Paxton, Decimus Burton, and Richard Turner favored a completely open design and perfected a model that could be adapted to both great tropical greenhouses built on curvilinear frames and more modest dwellings for the middle classes. With cast iron, wrought iron, and glass, all manner of extravagant forms could be realized; at the time, the vogue was for Moorish-inspired designs. In Stuttgart, for example, this style inspired King Wilhelm I of Württemberg, when he commissioned the architect Karl Ludwig von Zanta to build his summer residence, the Wilhelma (completed in 1854). It also inspired the great palm-tree greenhouses built by Karl Friedrich Schinkel in the 1830s for Friedrich Wilhelm III of Prussia on the outskirts of Berlin. A few years earlier, the Prince of Bohemia had constructed a conservatory to link his castle and his riding school. The architect Franz Beer, who was responsible for this work, drew his inspiration from cathedrals rather than Arab palaces.

In Paris, Princess Mathilde, daughter of Jérôme Bonaparte and niece of the Emperor, also dreamed of her own conservatory. It was designed as a large gallery adjoining the façade of her private mansion on the Rue de Courcelles, and could be reached from several different rooms. Ferns, palm trees, and various climbing plants grew there. Yet the few descriptions that have come down to us suggest that it was more like an exquisite reception room than a real greenhouse, with Turkish, Persian, and Afghan rugs, dragon-headed columns, Chinese or Japanese furniture, and Venetian crystal. The plants, all in pots, were arranged according to whether the gallery was to be the setting for a sumptuous dinner or was intended to resemble a sort of treasure trove. In other indoor gardens, the jungle effect was

Royal winter gardens expressed a love of travel and oriental tastes, and, in nineteenth-century Europe, they symbolized total freedom and the wildest exoticism (facing page, *The Palm Court of Friedrich Wilhelm III*, by Blechen, 1832, and above: *The Winter Garden of Saint Petersburg*, by M. Ivanovich, 1840).

enhanced by an even more theatrical décor. A series of articles appeared in praise of this fashion, inspired largely by images from *A Thousand and One Nights*.

Loudon's recommendations had appeared early in the century, but in 1852 Neumann (the director of the Paris Jardin des Plantes) gave a detailed description of the best way to design a conservatory that would correspond exactly to this popular idea of exoticism. He recommended, for example, creating an artistic effect by imitating the luxuriant disorder of a virgin forest, which would camouflage the structural elements. "We maintain that the following principle can still be applied to all kinds of greenhouse: wherever stonework is not essential, it must be considered detrimental, for there is always too much of it; it is in the best interest of greenhouse plants to replace stone with glass wherever possible." Neumann also took his inspiration from nature to design a new kind of glass roof, in which the panels were no longer arranged geometrically. As cast iron is easy to shape, he thought, why not create an informal criss-cross pattern, in imitation of the way real branches are interlaced, behind which the sky would appear to be within reach? Creepers would then twine themselves around this framework, forming garlands of foliage with bridges here and there, in the best possible imitation of a jungle. The columns and pilasters in this ideal winter garden would look like palm trees, and the overall magical effect would be even greater as the décor would look real. Nothing would be missing from this perfect environment: those privileged to enter would marvel at the sight of bridges, cascades, ornamental lakes with exotic fish, and calm shores strewn with clear gravel.

Certain connoisseurs, however, had not waited for Neumann's advice before creating their own theatrical décor. The concern for realism was such that servants were often dressed in the costumes of the countries that had inspired the garden. The smartest thing, however, was to have servants who came from those very countries: the exotic effect was then guaranteed.

None of these extravagant places, however, could beat the famous roof-garden that Ludwig II of Bavaria had built in 1867 in his royal residence in Munich. It was designed by the architect August von Voit to extend a first winter garden which was considered too cramped. This fabulous hanging garden was well suited to the king's naturally excessive nature. It was 650 feet (200 meters) long, 100 feet (30 meters) wide, and took four years to build. Phenomenal quantities of earth had to be hauled up and countless trees and other plants had to be transported and placed inside the steel and glass structure. The building itself was rather classical in style, and therefore quite a contrast to the general tone of the roof-garden. The architect was able to fulfill his master's dream of creating a magical Kashmiri valley. It was so huge that there was ample room to satisfy each royal whim: a cascade, a grotto, bridges, paths, a reed hut, a pagoda.

Ludwig II escaped from the real world by sailing through this artificial paradise in his little golden boat, surrounded by swans.

Here, all was in harmony: there were even musicians hidden among the foliage to accompany him on his way, and real birds flying past fake panoramas. On one side he could see the Himalayan peaks, on the other the vast plains of India. Ludwig II was usually alone in this wonderful oasis; he rarely invited any guests along, and as the only access to this garden was through his private apartments, certain eminent members of the court resorted to dressing up as common gardeners, which was the only way to get to the sacrosanct place! When the king died in 1886—drowned in the ornamental lake in the castle gardens—this folly was quickly demolished, to the relief, no doubt, of the apprentice cooks who had to carry umbrellas to reach their bedrooms on the floor below—apparently the waterfalls were not all completely leakproof.

Perhaps to give their passengers a foretaste of the foreign lands they were heading for, most ocean liners boasted glass-roofed gardens. Here is the first-class garden on the *Cap Arcona* (facing page, top).
Visiting Princess Mathilde at the Plaine Monceau in Paris was like setting out on a fantastic journey; her winter garden, with its gigantic plants, Turkish rugs, and Chinese furniture, was an exotic dream world (facing page, bottom).
Ludwig II of Bavaria was famous for his extravagance; the roof-garden he had built at his Munich residence (above) was the wildest of all imaginable follies.

Plants and fashions

Orange trees gave their name to the buildings that protected them, but no single plant was ever associated with the greenhouse. Since the days when these steel and glass structures first came into fashion, tastes in plants had been changing constantly. In the early nineteenth century, most amateur botanists simply wanted to use these ingenious shelters to grow plants early in the season; then they planted them out in the open ground once fine weather arrived. The influx of new plants offered new possibilities. The palm tree, of all the newcomers, generated the most excitement. In the 1830s the Loddiges brothers (who owned nurseries in Hackney, east of London) had no fewer than 160 varieties for sale in their catalogue. In just a few years, the palm tree acquired a unique status: it symbolized a certain lifestyle and an exotic elegance associated with the regions it came from. The search for a lost paradise, which had begun toward the end of the seventeenth century, was championed by the palm tree. Whereas landscape gardens or parks favored

Chinese pavilions, Egyptians pyramids, or Gothic chapels, the palm tree was given pride of place in most greenhouses: sitting in its striped shade, the visitor could dream of foreign lands or indulge in a nostalgic reverie. The palm tree never really lost its supremacy. At Bicton Gardens in Devon, the Palm House built about 1820 was based on Loudon's design; its structure and tiny panes of glass make it a particularly fine specimen, and it still gives some idea of the passion aroused by the palm tree.

Around 1850, other plant species from across the world also became very popular. The horticultural writer Charles Lemaire recorded this in particularly enthusiastic terms: "Why, a hothouse is tropical vegetation transported into our cold and cloudy climes!" The same man also wrote: "Is it not a truly great and beautiful thing to bring together, in the same small space, plants that grow in the four corners of the earth, some on mountains, others in valleys; some as parasites on trees, others in the water; from Hudson's Bay to Cape Horn, from the Atlas Mountains to the Cape of Good Hope, from Yemen to Japan, from Tibet to the Cape Province; and even

This impassive Buddha, half-hidden among the greenery, contributes to the peaceful atmosphere in this greenhouse (above). The Tropical Greenhouse at the Jardin des Plantes in Paris is like an impenetrable forest, with its tree ferns and huge philodendrons, among many other species (facing page).

Henri-Paul Nenot (1853–1934) drew these plans for an Athenaeum in a capital city, which was to include meeting rooms, a library, and a conservatory. "Why, a hothouse is tropical vegetation transported into our cold and cloudy climes!" exclaimed a horticultural writer, around 1850, in his enthusiasm for these plant species which had traveled across the world to be admired by visitors to greenhouses (facing page).

the myriad groups of islands dotted about the Pacific Ocean! . . . How pleasant it is, when the wintry ground is bare and desolate, when a blizzard is raging outside the window, when all is frosty outside and the rivers frozen over, to come and swell one's lungs in the sweet, warm atmosphere of the hothouse, to breathe in the heady fragrances of tropical orchids and Liliaceae from India and Cape Town, to see palm trees and huge banana leaves swaying above one's head."

These lyrical passages give us some idea of how the greenhouse was perceived in those days, as a fantastic means of escape into another world. An ever-growing number of enthusiasts were fascinated by these wonderful plants with their magical names, but they tended to focus on a single species, rather than trying to create artistic arrangements with several, as was the case later. Most people, therefore, used their greenhouses as botanists did: the plants were lined up in their pots and classified according to type. It was not until ferns came into fashion that things really changed.

In the latter half of the nineteenth century, ferns were the favorite temperate plants. They were collected avidly, as camellias would be later. "Ferneries" began to appear, in which a profusion of ferns and statues of all kinds were to be found, in less orderly arrangements than in the usual greenhouse. Moreover, the cultivation of ferns required the greenhouse to be organized differently, so its interior layout became less rigid. As this greenhouse was, by definition, a place where natural species were grown, efforts were made to banish all visible signs of human intervention. Straight lines gave way to meandering paths, where the visitor might chance upon some especially delightful variety of fern with lovely fronds of the most delicate hue. The notion of a "visit" to the greenhouse was gradually replaced by that of a pleasant stroll.

Today, Tatton Park in Cheshire is still the best example of this type of fernery. It has a particularly impressive collection of Australasian tree ferns, brought back by a member of the Egerton family (proprietors of the estate from the sixteenth century until 1958). Visiting the Tatton Park fern-ery (thought to have been built by Paxton) is like stepping into a humid, mysterious jungle.

Toward the 1860s, with the advent of subtropi-cal species, the purely botanical conception of the greenhouse had given way to a decidedly aesthetic approach. Crotons, caladiums, dracaenas, and all the plants with large, glossy leaves that we hardly notice today were then the height of fashion. They were either cleverly arranged or tangled around columns in a way that instantly evoked their native forests.

Fashions in greenhouse plants seem to have con-stantly wavered between a taste for the exotic and a deep-rooted affection for plants from more tem-perate regions. By the late nineteenth century, the vogue was for plants like rhododendrons, azaleas, camellias, and certain flowering plants that were already familiar but had not yet been seen in such diversity. Begonias and chrysanthemums were fine examples of the extraordinary dynamism of horti-cultural research. As these flowering plants grew in popularity, the interior of the greenhouse was rearranged.

Rather than large plants taking up the whole space, a central area was cleared, where visitors could converse at leisure, sitting in the comfort of armchairs. Pathways were no longer the fashion, but shelves were arranged around the edge of the greenhouse, where the plants could still be admired. This stricter arrangement also had the advantage of reducing heating costs and making maintenance easier. Modern conservatories are still designed along these lines. Just as the orangery had gradu-ally been diverted from its initial purpose, becom-ing a place for social gatherings, man made a sort of pact with the greenhouse, an *entente cordiale*,

according to which the plants no longer monopo-lized the place but were still there to delight the eye. These "mixed" conservatories bear little rela-tion to the strictly botanical hothouses used for the exclusive cultivation of plants—over the past hun-dred years, they have become places in which to relax, where plants are essentially decorative.

Glass Palaces

When the greenhouse first came into fashion, it was an object of admiration and a source of romantic inspiration. Yet these structures were associated with country houses or botanic gardens, as if they belonged only to parks or large gardens. From the early nineteenth century on, however, this notion began to change—especially after the 1840s, when these enchanting places made their first appearance in towns, and were no longer reserved for an elite but open to the general public.

The public greenhouse in Europe

Paris was the first city to boast an urban greenhouse. The Pont des Arts bridge, built between 1801 and 1803, was designed as a monument to the glory of cast iron: this versatile material could clearly be used for all manner of robust but elegant constructions. It was an instant success. Parisians flocked to the Pont des Arts, not just to cross the river, but also to linger and admire the sunset. Their enthusiasm was undoubtedly fired by the greenhouses on either side of the bridge, where they could admire all kinds of unusual little plants, displayed on shelves. The beauty of these magical surroundings was further enhanced by tubs planted with orange trees, bay trees, or hydrangeas. The entrance fee was considered money well spent.

A few decades later, there was another treat in store for Parisians: the first winter garden on the Champs-Élysées, a construction financed by private capital. Rohault de Fleury's greenhouses in the Jardin des Plantes inspired the design of a glass building, which would be used to display plants (some of which would be for sale) all year round: this building would include a tea room for refreshments. As soon as the resulting winter garden opened, in January 1846, it drew such crowds that an extension was required. It was a building of truly breathtaking proportions, designed exclusively for leisure activities. There was a ballroom, a huge café adjoining a reading room, a panorama of London scenes, several promenades, and a landscaped garden with lawns, flower beds, and fountains. Indeed, it was such a wonderful place that even Victor Hugo was in raptures: "summer has been captured under glass," he wrote, a feeling shared by everyone. A year later, he wrote a second admiring article, after attending a ball in this "huge iron cage. . . the size of four or five cathedrals, all enclosed in glass . . . On entering, one was dazzled by the flood of light; through this brilliance, one could make out all sorts of magnificent flowers and strange trees, with

In the seventeenth century, there were no greenhouses in towns. Throughout the following century, however, they arrived *en masse*, to the delight of city-dwellers. Crowds flocked to the little greenhouses on the Pont des Arts (below), or the vast winter garden on the Champs-Élysées (facing page, top). A collection for the poor, beneath the splendid chandeliers of a magnificent winter garden (facing page, bottom). In Brussels, spectacular greenhouses were built in the Palais Royal grounds at Laeken (page 56).

the leaves and forms of the tropics and Florida: banana trees, palm trees, latanias [that is, different kinds of palm], cedars, large leaves, huge thorns, strange twisted branches, intermingled as in a virgin forest." The miracle was that this seemingly make-believe world was in fact real: the plants were real and the water in the fountains was real—and the whole magical environment was contained within an area as large as a park, in which a summer atmosphere reigned all year round. Every detail was perfect, right down to the scent of orange blossom and the trill of birds. Paxton, who had designed the famous Chatsworth Conservatory for the Duke of Devonshire, was invited to a concert here in 1848,

and he too was bewitched by the atmosphere of this garden on the Champs-Élysées. He had not yet constructed the building that was to make him famous: London's extraordinary Crystal Palace.

Across the English Channel, the city of Glasgow also treated itself to the luxury of a winter garden. It was designed by the Scottish architect John Kibble, who had been influenced by Loudon's work on curvilinear greenhouses. The building he produced had two domes, one bigger than the other, both covered in green glass. Inside, apart from the usual rare plants, visitors could admire a dozen different varieties of araucaria (that is, monkey puzzle trees) imported directly from South America, as well as the largest flowering dracaena ever seen "in captivity." But the real jewel of Kibble Palace was just under the great dome: an impressive ornamental pond with an island on which Kibble had reproduced Greek and Roman ruins. Scale models of ships coasted around the island, towed by a steam-powered tug. Among the 4,000 visitors who flocked to its inauguration in 1865, there must have been a lot of wide-eyed children, amazed by this extraordinary sight!

Kibble Palace was originally built alongside the river. It was certainly thanks to John Kibble's foresight that it was spared the fate of many other

winter gardens, which proved so costly that they were dismantled one by one. Kibble's family did not share his passion for plants, and he sensed that they could not be depended upon to care for them. He therefore made a financial arrangement with the Glasgow Botanic Garden: the directors of the garden agreed to take the building over on Kibble's death. Kibble Palace moved to a new site and was enlarged: today it boasts a fine collection of tropical plants and a wonderful variety of tree ferns. The statues that nestle among the greenery seem to hold their breath, hardly daring to believe that this paradise has survived the passing of time.

The larger of the Palace's two domes is a splendid example of what contemporary architects most admired. It is over 130 feet (40 meters) in diameter, and was designed in two parts: an upper section built on a frame supported by twelve columns, and a lower section held on twenty-four finely carved columns. There are ventilation and spraying systems at strategic points, either where the two sections of the dome meet or in the lower section's glass walls.

During the last three decades of the nineteenth century, many of these elegant glass structures were erected throughout Europe to display fine selections of exotic plants. The greenhouse built in Copenhagen by Rothe and Jacobsen (1874) was in large part inspired by Kibble Palace. This same year, the city of Florence acquired a Palm Grove in the Orto Botanico. Similar buildings sprang up in Madrid (1887), Liverpool (1896), and Berlin (1907), like proud emblems of these cities' advance into an age of progress and prosperity. Near Vienna, Emperor Franz Joseph had what

In the Glasgow Botanic Garden,
the glass of Kibble Palace has survived
the winters of a century and a half
intact, substantiating
the arguments in favor of curvilinear
structures (above).
The greenhouses in Lyon's Parc
de la Tête d'Or are still the city's pride
(facing page, top and bottom).
A visit to this extraordinary garden,
with its thousands of species,
is like a botanical world tour.

turned out to be the last of the great Palm Houses built in the grounds of the fabulous palace of Schönbrunn in 1880.

The town greenhouse now began to flourish. The architect Hector Horeau finished the construction of the Château des Fleurs in the French city of Lyon less than six months before the inauguration of the second winter garden on the Champs-Elysées. Visitors to this Castle of Flowers were astounded by its size and beauty: they could wander from the tropical greenhouse to the ladies' salon, then linger in the reading room before moving on to the

children's room, generally considered the highlight of the visit. Two other greenhouses also demonstrated Horeau's vision of nature and architecture in harmony, and he dreamed of recreating the success of Lyon on a much grander scale. But such plans were expensive, and his ideas for a boulevard winter garden in Paris were shelved.

Lyon distinguished itself again with the Parc de la Tête d'Or in 1857. On 1,235 acres (500 hectares) of land, the landscape architects Denis and Eugène Bühler created an artificial lake and a first greenhouse of 3,770 square feet (350 square meters). Other greenhouses followed: at first they were made of wood, but in 1875 they were rebuilt in cast iron on an iron framework. Placed side by side, these ribbed greenhouses eventually covered an area of 53,800 square feet (5,000 square meters). The Lyon botanic garden was already on the site of the Parc de la Tête d'Or: the Bühler brothers integrated it into their design, and the new greenhouses expanded its existing collections. There are five greenhouses in all, each of which specializes in plants suited to a particular climate. One greenhouse is reserved for carnivorous plants, and there are hot and temperate houses that shelter respectively bromeliads, aroids, orchids, ferns, and dazzling arrangements of chrysanthemums, cyclamens, and azaleas. The largest greenhouse, 66 feet high by 98 feet long (20 meters high by 30 meters long) is reserved for the tropical garden and the cultivation of camellias, some of which are almost as old as the park itself.

Beneath the dome of Kibble Palace, in the middle of a forest of tropical ferns, this half-naked beauty seems to look modestly away as the indiscreet visitor approaches (right).
The Atiocha station in the heart of Madrid is a reminder of the era when architecture worked miracles with steel and glass (facing page).

Paxton's travels developed his taste for exotic plants. When his name was not associated with the greenhouses he designed (below and facing page, the Flintham conservatory in England), it was connected to a great variety of plant species. The *Victoria regia* waterlily was one of his favorites (left), for which he built a special greenhouse at Chatsworth.

Finally, the hot and humid atmosphere of the greenhouse aquarium is home to impressive Amazonian specimens. This hothouse replaced the *Victoria regia* greenhouse (1887), which was unfortunately destroyed in 1980. The *Victoria regia* waterlily comes from Guyana; it had such trouble becoming acclimatized to Kew Gardens that Joseph Paxton took one to Chatsworth, where it thrived to such an extent that soon there were over a hundred flowers, with leaves 5 feet (1.5 meters) in diameter. These leaves, with their alternating solid and hollow veins, were extremely strong: Paxton demonstrated this by sitting his seven-year-old daughter on one of them. They also inspired him to build a new kind of greenhouse, the "Victoria," for the exclusive cultivation of these wonderful Guyanese plants. The *Victoria regia* greenhouse in the Parc de la Tête d'Or was shaped like a rotunda, and contained a circular pool 26 feet (8 meters) in diameter. There was a sidewalk 3 feet (1 meter) wide all around it, from which gardeners could tend the huge plants and visitors could admire them.

The Crystal Palace: a heroic achievement

Of all the mid-nineteenth-century monuments to the glory of glass and steel, the Crystal Palace had the greatest impact. It has gone down in history as a feat of great daring, building such a palace in the very heart of London. The project originated in January 1850, when Prince Albert called for the creation of a single building that could display all the symbols of British superiority in trade and industry during the 1851 Universal Exhibition. Architects were quite unprepared for this request, and a good number of ambitious projects were disqualified through lack of time. The weeks passed, and it began to look extremely unlikely that the prince's wish would be fulfilled.

In early June, Paxton was informed of the difficulties encountered by the committee in charge of judging the various projects. At that time, Paxton was known mostly for his talents as a gardener and collector of rare plants. He had built the Great Conservatory at Chatsworth for his patron the Duke of Devonshire, but there was no possible comparison between that construction and the plans for an enormous glass building he submitted to the

Royal Commission on June 22, 1850. Although several members of the committee were openly skeptical, they hardly had time to think things over. When they accepted Paxton's project nearly three weeks later, they were taking a genuine risk. The Kew and Chatsworth conservatories were certainly elegant, harmonious structures, but this was something totally different. The miracle was, however, achieved: the superb transparent cathedral, with its 891,000 square feet (82,800 square meters) of glass, 3,300 cast-iron columns, and 600,270 cubic feet (17,000 cubic meters) of wood, sprang up in only a few months, in time to astound the world when the Universal Exhibition was inaugurated on May 1, 1851. The record number of visitors testifies to the exceptional nature of the event and the curiosity it aroused. Between its inauguration and the end of the Exhibition on October 15, 1851, about six million visitors crowded into this unique palace, 1,840 feet (560 meters) long, which could have comfortably contained four basilicas the size of St. Peter's in Rome.

Technological progress was certainly encouraging, but was it good enough for the construction of Paxton's giant in steel and glass? And was it reasonable to entrust a gardener with the building of this Crystal Palace (facing page, bottom) when an architect or engineer might have seemed more appropriate?
Another crystal palace of the past: the greenhouses in the botanical gardens in the southern part of London's Hyde Park; visitors reported that they were ablaze with the bright colors of azaleas, orchids, and roses (above and facing, top).

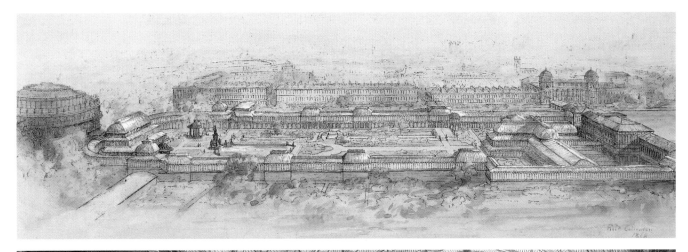

The committee in charge
of selecting the projects for
the Universal Exhibition of 1851
had expressed their doubts—yet
the whole world was amazed
by the Crystal Palace on its
inauguration day (left).
Refreshments, by L. Nagne,
skillfully reflects the extraordinary
impression Paxton's masterpiece
must have made on its visitors
(facing page).

The Universal Exhibition itself was intended to glorify colonialism and the reign of Queen Victoria, but the real hero was Paxton, who had erected a monumental, magical temple in record time, without sacrificing elegance. This example was undoubtedly a deciding factor in the rapid development of greenhouses of all shapes and sizes in the following years. With steel, glass, and wood, Paxton had managed to create a grandiose, luminous monument, which became an inspiration to many designers. It had taken thirty-two weeks to build the Crystal Palace in Hyde Park. It hardly took longer

These indolent sphinxes seem perfectly at home in their sumptuous surroundings, as though they imagine themselves back in ancient Egypt. Delamotte took these photographs of the Crystal Palace, after its transfer to Sydenham Hill. They give a clear idea of the work involved in reconstructing it (above and facing page, bottom).

to dismantle it and move it to Sydenham Hill. in the south of London. After its second inauguration in June 1854. it was divided into several areas, including an orangery, a tropical greenhouse, a concert hall, and several restaurants. This symbol of British prosperity came to a tragic end in November 1936, when it was completely destroyed by fire.

How could the organizers of the Paris Exhibition in 1867 outdo Paxton's achievement in London?

Napoleon III did not even try to compete with the size of the Crystal Palace. but instead decided to challenge the British model in terms of elegance. Fifteen beautifully ornate greenhouses and winter gardens were therefore built on the site of the Champs-Élysées gardens, where the public could admire a magnificent collection of rare plants in suitably splendid surroundings. The following Exhibitions (in 1878, 1889, and 1900) continued to celebrate the magical association of glass and metal. in structures that let the clear morning light filter beautifully through the delicate patterns of palm trees and ferns. Unfortunately, the extraordinary notoriety of the tower built by the engineer Alexandre Gustave Eiffel for the Universal Exhibition of 1889 rather distracted attention from the horticultural palace, in the 272-foot (83-meter) long greenhouses built on either side of the Cours Albert I.

The Palais des Congrès at the Universal Exhibition of 1900 in Paris looks like a gigantic liner moored alongside the river (above).

The American greenhouse

Paxton's Crystal Palace seems to have been the inspiration for many magnificent constructions, first in Europe, then in America. Paxton contributed a plan for the First American Exhibition, held in New York in 1854, but it was not selected. The final project, drawn up by the architects Carstensen and Gilde- meister, was nevertheless strongly reminiscent of the Palace in Hyde Park that had drawn such enthusiastic crowds. The New York building was more ornate and finely worked, with a roof that was half-transparent, half-opaque. Sadly, it also succumbed to fire, only five years after its creation.

America certainly lagged behind Europe in terms of greenhouses; one of the reasons is that while Europe was already debating the respective merits of rectilinear or curvilinear structures, there were still very few public parks in American cities. The Boston public park, created in 1839, was the exception that proved the rule, as the plans for New York's Central Park were not drawn up for another twenty years (1859). By then, any self-respecting park had to have a greenhouse; the Central Park

design therefore included plans for a glass building that would shelter rare plant species. The design of this Flower Conservatory was similar to that of the Palm House in Kew Gardens.

Andrew Jackson Downing initiated the idea of Central Park; after his death the scheme was carried out by the landscape architect Frederick Law Olmsted with a team includ- ing Calvert Vaux, who was British, and his assistant J. Wrey Mould. While traveling through England, Downing had been impressed by the didactic nature of the great British greenhouses, of which he considered Kew to be the finest example. The American plan, therefore, also aimed to amaze and entertain the visitor while adding to his knowledge of botany. If the greenhouse first designed had ever existed, it would have been a rather classical cruci- form model, with a curvilinear structure—but the greenhouse that was finally built in 1899 testified to the authorities' preference for rectilinear structures. Until it was demolished in 1934, it was one of New Yorkers' favorite places, with its palm trees and exotic species that could beckon summer from the very depths of winter.

In 1889, two young American botanists, Nathaniel Lord Britton and his wife, made a trip to Kew Gardens, an inspiration for the ambitious project for the New York Botanical Garden in the Bronx (above).

The Americans succumbed
to the charm of the greenhouse later
than the Europeans, but they then
adopted it with passionate enthusiasm
(left, the Longwood conservatory;
below, the Wave Hill conservatory
in New York state).

In fact, Philadelphia was the first American city to boast a real winter garden. It was built by Hermann J. Schwarzmann and completed in 1876, and its style was a cross between Gothic and Moorish. It was part of a series of buildings designed to celebrate the city's centenary, and it was described as the most spectacular garden ever built under glass. It was inspired by European examples, but extra attention was paid to color and ornamentation. Visitors were treated to a great diversity of splendid sights, including sumptuous Victorian flower beds, aquatic gardens, and marble fountains. But they were also able to discover countless fascinating details about the virtues of the medicinal or exotic plants so beautifully displayed. This glass palace was demolished in 1955.

America followed the European lead, and greenhouses began to appear in many cities. These charmingly convivial places sprang up everywhere: from Detroit to Baltimore (the Druid Hill Park conservatory, completed in 1888, is a copy of the Palm House built in Vienna for the 1873 Exhibition), Chicago, and Cleveland. A scheme was launched for an American version of the famous Palm House in Kew Gardens, to be built in the New York Botanical Garden in the Bronx. The architect appointed was William R. Cobb, who was also an admirer of the Crystal Palace; he hired the famous Lord & Burnham Company to construct the building according to his plans. The style of this greenhouse was strongly influenced by the Italian Renaissance, which had been showcased at the 1893 Chicago Exhibition. In 1978, a major restoration project was initiated (thanks to a generous donation from Enid A. Haupt), which enabled the public to rediscover the finest American example of the Victorian greenhouse.

Most of the original features of the greenhouse have been eliminated, however: the most recent restoration, completed in 1997, was based on the oldest sketches still existing, which date from the 1930s.

The present greenhouse is topped with a rotunda 98 feet (30 meters) in diameter, bearing a dome 82 feet (25 meters) high, and extended to left and right by five galleries, several of which are embellished with cruciform pavilions. Two other curving greenhouses complete the ensemble.

Visitors can discover the infinite variety of plants that grow in the world's different climates. In the space of a few feet they can travel the world, from tropical Mexican forests to the deserts of Africa, from Brazilian rainforests to the subtropical regions of Australia. Among the 3,000 plants on show, some originate from specimens that featured in the Botanical Garden's 1902 inaugural catalog. Finally, two huge galleries are reserved for temporary exhibitions, which draw large crowds every year, with such themes as rare plants, useful plants (mahogany, sugar cane, or the precious palm tree *Cocos nucifera*) and surprising or simply splendid plants. Like all gardens of this type, the Bronx one takes its teaching role very seriously. Visitors can glean useful information by observing trunks, leaf patterns or textures, and the park schedules programs intended to heighten public awareness of ecological and environmental issues.

Since its creation, the Bronx's Great Conservatory has had to be restored six times, mostly because of the corrosive effects of the New York climate on the combination of glass, wood, and metal that makes up the structure. The latest improvements were made in 1997, and apart from the total reconstruction of the greenhouses and the replacement of 17,000 sheets of glass, an ultra-sophisticated computer system was installed to ensure the perfect control of temperature, humidity, and ventilation. Thanks to these innovations, the New York Botanical Garden boasts one of the world's most spectacular "plant havens."

The New York Botanical Garden was originally financed by such notable personalities as J. P. Morgan, Cornelius Vanderbilt, and Andrew Carnegie; successive restorations have given new luster to this gigantic ensemble (previous double page and above). Under the huge sun-drenched vault, a stone's throw from the effervescence of New York, the palm trees whisper tales of Africa (facing page).

Kew, Laeken: royal passions

Of the many greenhouses that were created in the second half of the nineteenth century, two absolute jewels still exist. One was built for a king, the other for a group of royal gardens turned into a national institution, and they are elegant demonstrations that the dreams of the powerful sometimes resemble those of ordinary men.

Crystal Palace was renowned for its size. The Palm House at Kew Gardens (in Surrey, in the southern part of London) is also large, but crowds of visitors still flock to the gardens primarily to admire its grace and elegance. The directors of the Royal Botanic Gardens at Kew, anxious to satisfy the popular demand for palm trees, decided to construct a building worthy of housing a fine collection. Two architects, Richard Turner (1798–1881) and Decimus Burton (1800–1881), were consulted. Although the former pretended to bow down to the latter's suggestions, it was only so that he could later change the plans as he pleased once construction was under way (between 1844 and 1848).

This rivalry reflected the importance attached to the greenhouse as a symbol of modernity: it resulted in a structure that gives an extraordinary impression of lightness. The cast- and wrought-iron frame looks as delicate as a fine transparent shell, and seems to literally float on a stone base just under 3 feet (1 meter) high. At its widest, it measures 98 feet (30 meters), at its longest 360 feet (110 meters), and its maximum height of 66 feet (20 meters) enables it to shelter the tallest palm trees in the collection. Banana trees, ginger, and impressive rubber plants also thrive in this hot, humid environment. Richard Turner's rather underhanded methods were partly responsible for the construction of this gem, erected to the glory of transparency. It was an incomparable symbol of the contemporary fascination with glass.

The Temperate House, which was constructed a few years later for the same gardens at Kew, is quite different. This work was wholly assigned to Decimus Burton, and was at first destined to house Australian, Chilean, and Mexican garden plants. For a long time, it was unfavorably compared

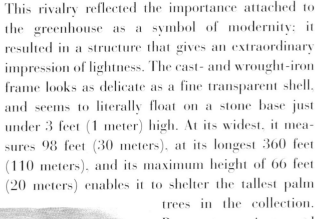

The London sun shines into the Kew Gardens greenhouses, masterpieces of harmony and elegance (facing page). The framework designed by Turner was three times lighter than Burton's. It still attracts admiring crowds (above, the Palm House). In 1895, the colored glass of the Palm House at Kew was replaced by transparent glass, better suited to the health of the plants than the original greenish tint (following double page).

with the Palm House; but since its renovation in 1982 it has been reinstated and is now much admired for its elegance. Burton's greenhouse consists of a central pavilion flanked by two smaller ones, and demonstrates the architect's preference for ventilation systems through the roof. Many plant species thrive in this perfect environment, protected from the climatic variations that would otherwise be lethal. Apart from many tea plants, dragon trees, and lemon trees, there are elegant daturas, all kinds of begonias, and huge skyward-climbing creepers. The Kew Temperate House is also home to a sumptuous cypress from Kashmir, whose delicate bluish top almost touches the roof.

The huge constructions at Kew beg the question, does the greenhouse exist for the greater comfort of plants or of men? The Palm House is as pure in outline as an igloo, and as impressive in size as a cathedral. It was specifically designed by Burton and Turner to satisfy all the requirements of tender, demanding plants. The skillful balance of heat, light, and space is calculated to suit many varieties of palm trees. And although the architecture is spectacular, it does not correspond to an ideal as regards human habitation. The rectilinear design of the Temperate House, however, is closer to such

an ideal. The square structure, with its stone pillars and sloping walls, looks more like a huge temple or a princely palace than a building designed solely to shelter a collection of frost-fearing plants.

There are so many wonderful greenhouses in the world that it would be impossible to establish a hierarchy, but those lucky enough to visit the sumptuous Royal Conservatories at Laeken during the brief periods when they are open must feel themselves privileged to enter the most remarkable example

An enchanting floral passage in the Laeken conservatories, which are open to visitors for only ten days a year (facing page). The magnificent collections in the various Kew conservatories are constantly being expanded (below, the Temperate House which shelters lemon trees, tea plants, and dragon trees). Modern greenhouses, like the Princess of Wales Conservatory (above), have been added.

Leopold II dreamed of transforming Laeken into a botanical wonderland: under a glass shelter, the visitor would discover treasure after treasure as he went from one garden to the next. These gardens would be created in a series of "rooms," linked to each other by passages full of flowers. The sovereign's dream was fulfilled: in 1876, the Laeken ensemble was built according to plans drawn up by the architect Auguste Balat. It consists of an orangery, a dining room, a series of greenhouses for camellias, rhododendrons, azaleas, or palm trees, a fernery, a little theater, the Congo greenhouse, and the winter garden itself. The structure is remarkable in every way: it is resolutely curvilinear, and despite its impressive size it looks surprisingly light, and seems almost to be floating above the ground—an impression that is due largely to the fact that the glass is placed inside the steel structure. On top of the Palm House is a huge rotunda divided into domes, reminiscent of the Kibble Palace in Glasgow.

No columns distract the eye inside this greenhouse. The beautifully decorated arches that support the rotunda from the outside, running the length of the roof, look more like decorative elements than indispensable parts of the structure. The crown that tops the dome is a reminder that this is a royal building. In 1876, a chapel greenhouse was designed, also topped with a dome, and completed with a series of eight smaller peripheral chapels used for religious services. Leopold III, who was a less pious

of all. So many fabulous buildings with such varied collections of plants are breathtaking indeed. King Leopold II (1835–1909) instigated this magnificent project: when he came to the throne in 1865 at the age of thirty, he was already very interested in biology in general and in plants in particular. At the time, the Laeken botanical garden had only a simple orangery and a fairly small, round greenhouse, which in no way corresponded to Leopold II's dream of a garden worthy of his passion for rare plants. The king's frequent travels in North Africa, India, and China stoked this passion, and thanks to Belgium's colonial interests in the Congo, there was no lack of a supply of them.

In Belgium's Laeken garden, there are thirty-six greenhouses under 10 acres (4 hectares) of glass. The magnificent plant collection takes up 5 acres (2 hectares), and the whole site is like a fabulous glass city. The 82-foot (25-meter) dome on its thirty-six Doric columns is breathtaking (above and facing page).

(or perhaps more athletic) monarch, had these chapels converted into a swimming pool.

Visiting the Royal Laeken greenhouses in May is a unique opportunity to admire one of the world's most extraordinary collections of azaleas. A great deal of devoted care still goes into the upkeep of these greenhouses; indeed, it seems as if Leopold II's passion for rare plants has been handed down through the generations. The atmosphere in this Belgian greenhouse is such that, when gazing up through the palm trees, one could believe oneself in Africa.

In Austria, the emperor Franz Joseph commissioned the architect Franz von Sengenschmid to design a series of greenhouses for the grounds of the fabulous Schönbrunn castle. These were completed in 1880, after only 15 months of building, and included the last—and biggest—of the great

European palm houses. They give an astonishing impression of lightness and transparency (again, the glass is inside the metal structure), and seem to belong to some oriental dream world, moored to earth by a garland of twisting, flowery creepers.

The Palm House in the Schönbrunn botanic garden in Keine, Austria, looks extraordinarily light and airy among the clipped yew trees. The sun streams in through its finely worked metal frame (above and facing page).

Collectors of rare plants

An extraordinary climate of creativity flourished at certain European courts, and found some expression in the construction of greenhouses. This passion was communicated to several aristocratic families, who also caught the virus for collecting rare plants and then needed somewhere to house them: a place in which the seasons could be tamed and the tropics transported to one's own garden. Such famous and wealthy families as the Rothschilds, the Perrier-Jouët champagne dynasty, and the Schneiders, manufacturers of Le Creuset cast-iron cookware, were impressed by buildings like the greenhouses in the Jardin des Plantes, Crystal Palace, Kew Gardens, or the famous winter gardens on the Champs-Élysées, and they too yielded to the temptation to create a paradise under a glass roof. Each individual had his own ideas regarding size, style, and ornamentation, but all were driven by a common desire to see jasmine flower in December or grapes ripen in spring. It was like having the powers of a magician in a world of mere mortals.

In Miriam Rothschild's book devoted to her family's parks and gardens, she writes that they were largely renowned for their greenhouses, which housed many wonderful species in their protective atmosphere.

Before the 1848 Revolution, Salomon de Rothschild (older brother of James, founder of the Parisian bank) had bought a house on the tip of the Suresnes island of Puteaux, just outside Paris. The mansion itself was completely destroyed during the uprising, but the greenhouses survived. They were used to cultivate both exotic plants and fruit and vegetables, and were rather classical in style; the largest, which was 131 feet (40 meters) long and 43 feet (13 meters) wide, was reserved for ornamental plants. It had a maximum height of 23 feet (7 meters), so it could hold camellias as tall as trees, as well as azaleas and extremely rare varieties of rhododendrons. The fruit and vegetables were grown in 300 frames spread over 650 feet (200 meters). Thanks to the zeal of a devoted team of gardeners, Salomon de Rothschild and his guests could enjoy cherries, peaches, figs, apricots, plums, and even pineapples long before their season.

Salomon's bother, James de Rothschild, will always be associated with the Château de Ferrières, which he bought in 1818 and which belonged to the family until 1978. James's nephew Meyer had introduced him to Paxton, who designed an imposing square structure for Ferrières, with a magnificent salon in a central courtyard under a glass roof. From the castle, romantic walks led to the imposing

At Miriam Rothschild's home in Ashton Wold, Northamptonshire, cowslips, primroses, and lady's smock create a delicate spring-like symphony.

Nearly all the Rothschilds have shared a passion for greenhouses; in the 1920s, these greenhouses at Ashton Wold sheltered hundreds of orchids.

greenhouses and winter garden. The baron adored rare plants, and his collection of orchids at Ferrières became famous.

Nearly every member of the Rothschild family has taken an interest in gardens, parks, and plants of all kinds. The most remarkable of all the Rothschild parks is Tring, in Hertfordshire (now an outpost of the Natural History Museum in London). In 1872, Lionel de Rothschild bought it as a wedding present for his eldest son Natty; at that time, it covered 5,000 acres (2,000 hectares). Natty instantly fell in love with this magical place, and devoted a lot of time to its greenhouses, fruit cages, and kitchen garden. His special favorite was the orchid greenhouse, which contained up to 2,000 plants, some of which were new varieties obtained by crossing the finest specimens. In her book, Miriam Rothschild also evokes another greenhouse, from which all the flowers were sent to Queen Mary every year on her birthday.

Another fine estate is Ashton Wold, in Northamptonshire, with its 625 acres (250 hectares) of wood, its rose garden, and its huge greenhouses. Charles de Rothschild settled there at the age of twenty; he had come across this enchanting place by accident, and was amazed to discover that this rather neglected estate belonged to his father, the famous Natty of Tring Park. Charles had fond childhood memories of the many greenhouses on the family estate at Tring, and decided to have similar ones built. He was especially proud of his cattleyas (a breed of orchid, immortalized by Proust in his novel *Swann in Love*). Their exquisite, pure white blooms were particularly highly valued at the time.

Charles made many discoveries on his botanical expeditions, including the blue waterlily *Nymphaea caerulea*, which required particular care. He had a special greenhouse built, in which two tanks 23 by 6 feet (7 by 2 meters) were hollowed out and filled with rain-water. The walls of the greenhouse were covered with ferns and other plants, so that the only light came from above.

Former orangeries are often used as reception rooms; left, the Moët et Chandon champagne house's orangery in Epernay dates from the early nineteenth century. Members of the Imperial court often stopped here on their way to Germany or Russia.

After Charles's death in 1923, many of his collections were distributed among England's most famous botanic gardens. Kew was the main beneficiary: 350 orchids were added to its collection, including fifteen varieties of cattleya. Thanks to the enthusiasm of its present owners, the magnificent Ashton estate is now devoted to the protection of wild flowers, the propagation of which reflects a renewed balance between flora and fauna. Although the greenhouses no longer contain the rarest orchids, these huge, glass cathedrals among the rose trees, lilacs, and wisteria are full of precious memories.

No description of the Rothschilds' gardens would be complete without a visit to Prégny. When Adolph de Rothschild bought this estate near Geneva in 1857 it was just a large piece of land, but Joseph Paxton (and his son-in-law George Stokes) stepped in to work wonders here too. Elizabeth of Austria, better known as Sissi, who often visited Prégny, was more sensitive than most to the beauty of the aviary and greenhouses, the biggest of which, 165 feet (50 meters) long, housed an extraordinary collection of exotic plants. These greenhouses now belong to the Geneva Botanic Garden. The Rothschild example is proof—if indeed any was needed—that every large estate had to have at least one greenhouse to have any prestige in the eyes of a society that had witnessed the miracle of the Crystal Palace.

Other wealthy families succumbed to the same passion. Champagne manufacturer M. Perrier-Jouët, for example, cultivated twenty-eight varieties of pineapple in his Epernay greenhouses and owned a vast rotunda that sheltered a family of palm trees. In 1880, the Schneider family erected greenhouses that were soon overflowing with orchids and begonias.

The town of Le Creuset (from which the Schneiders took the name for their wares) later bought the house and park in which these greenhouses stand, and now they have a dual function: to house permanent collections, and to produce the ornamental species that decorate the town.

These wealthy families helped to perpetuate the fashion for greenhouses. Industrial progress had resulted in the rise of a middle class, for whom a greenhouse was one of the essential outward signs of success: any self-respecting person had to have a piece of land on which to build a house and a greenhouse. The middle classes could now choose their greenhouses from catalogues. Certain contemporary figures, who were not necessarily rich, viewed these glass structures as a means of escaping into a dream world. In 1856, Victor Hugo bought a house in Guernsey, in which he had a conservatory built on the first floor and a greenhouse on the third, instead of the original attic. Hugo used to write there, standing near a white earthenware stove: it gave him a wonderful view of the sky, and on a clear day he could make out the pale outline of the French coast . . . a consolation to him in his exile.

In Boulogne-sur-Seine, just outside Paris, financier Albert Kahn owned 20 acres (8 hectares)

of land, in which he made his childhood dream come true. Kahn was an insatiably curious, self-taught businessman, and a believer in world peace. He took advantage of his travels and his love of plants to create a garden in which a variety of styles existed side by side. A French-style formal garden led to the oriental atmosphere of a delightful Japanese garden, for example. The surviving greenhouse is an elegant palm house, with a dome and a beautifully ornate door. Today's visitors can pause for refreshment in this oasis, so close to the bustle of the city: it is an idyllic place for lunch or tea.

Victor Hugo was most impressed by the winter garden on the Champs-Élysées. No doubt it influenced him when he transformed the attic of his Guernsey house (above)— and perhaps his imagination conjured up for him here the "satyrs, naked nymphs, and hydra" that he had admired in the famous Parisian garden.
Albert Kahn had a vast palm house built in his garden on the banks of the Seine. Nowadays it is a tea room, and very popular for Sunday lunch (left).

The great Auteuil greenhouse

Before 1854, Paris had no municipal plant nurseries to supply the city's parks and gardens. This was quite simply because, at that time, there were no public parks as such in Paris. When Parisians went out for a walk, they depended on the goodwill of the owners of royal residences, who cultivated their own plants.

The first municipal nursery was established in the Clos George (near the Porte de la Muette) on an area of nearly 7.5 acres (3 hectares). This first nursery proved insufficient, however, as more and more flowers and ornamental plants were needed for the parks and gardens that flourished throughout the Second Empire. A new site was needed, which would be big enough for present requirements and could later be extended. In 1898, the nursery was transferred to a 22.5-acre (9-hectare) site on the edge of the Bois de Boulogne. Jean-Camille Formigé (appointed architect of the "City of Paris Promenades and Plantations" in 1885) was given the job of developing this rather uneven terrain. The mound of earth alongside the avenue of the Porte d'Auteuil was transformed into a terrace leading to the garden.

Wide steps now lead from this terrace to a huge lawn, on each side of which are two groups of three greenhouses, each measuring 2,150 square feet (200 square meters). It's impossible to miss the Great Conservatory: it is 325 feet (99 meters) long, 39 feet (12 meters) wide, and almost 26 feet (8 meters) high. The 49-foot (15-meter) high Palm House dome towers over the ensemble. Other greenhouses consist entirely of frames that can be opened. There are sixty-four of these "pelargonium houses," and they bring the total area under glass to nearly 129,200 square feet (12,000 square meters)— double that of the first nursery at La Muette.

Formigé designed his greenhouses without any interior supports, to ensure maximum light inside and to allow the gardeners to move about freely. He also perfected a heating system of which he was very proud. An ingenious mechanism circulated hot water: the main innovation was that this water was not heated by boilers but by steam, conveyed through an impressive network of underground pipes. Thanks to heat exchangers at the entrance to each greenhouse, the water circulated at the required temperature through the entire length of the structure.

Thousands of visitors come every year to admire the strelitzias, banana trees, Egyptian papyrus, and *Victoria regia* in Jean-Camille Formigé's huge Tropical Greenhouse at the former municipal nurseries in Auteuil (facing page). In summer, the orange trees emerge from the greenhouses in their Versailles tubs to perfume the garden's paths (above).

The Auteuil greenhouses have just celebrated their centenary. Nowadays, visitors come either to the temporary exhibitions (such as a recent one on palm trees), or simply to enjoy a delightful stroll in the park. Horticultural production has moved to Rungis, south of Paris, where 322,800 square feet (30,000 square meters) of greenhouses and 100 acres (40 hectares) of tree nurseries produce three million plants for flower beds.

The kind of cultivation under glass that is practiced in Europe these days is exemplified by huge expanses in the Netherlands, which supply flowers to most European countries. These geraniums, begonias, azaleas, and fuchsias are now so common that it is difficult to imagine how rare they were just a hundred years ago.

The wealth of flowers that exists today is due to the invention of greenhouses. They experienced a spectacular rise, followed by an equally spectacular fall in popularity. They will forever be associated with great botanical expeditions and the remarkable technical progress of the nineteenth century—but when they fell out of favor, just before the First World War, they were rejected as suddenly as they had once been admired.

Several factors explain this decline. The first was the Romantic movement, which advocated a return to natural values and was afraid of industrial progress (the association of iron and glass was a direct result of this progress). The second was that the extremely wealthy class was losing certain privileges, including that of idleness, and they therefore had less time to devote to greenhouses. The third was a waning interest in tender, exotic plants, while a growing minority of people claimed that they were not worth the time and trouble, and were no more remarkable than any common or garden rose.

The Auteuil greenhouse is a surprisingly delicate iron and glass structure. It contains a palm house, a tropical greenhouse, and an exhibition center. It faces due south and gets plenty of sunlight (above). There is also an aviary (facing, a replica of the palm house), full of chattering parrots and budgerigars.

New greenhouses for a new millennium

Each succeeding generation compares its work to the past, incorporating lessons as well as possible. New theories are developed and progress continues.

A surprising and innovative example is the greenhouse 39 feet (12 meters) underground, at the Gare de Lyon, Paris. Travelers on Paris's newest metro line "Météor" are amazed to come across 6,300 square feet (585 square meters) of tropical rainforest. Every detail of this humid, luxuriant setting was minutely planned by its designer, François Tribel, and his associate Liliane Grünig. The result is a spectacular imitation of nature, with an hourly shower of tropical rain that really seems to fall from the sky. The cycads, palm trees, and tree ferns seem unaware of their cramped quarters, and are visibly thriving.

In spring of the year 2000, the Welsh Botanic Garden inaugurated a gigantic greenhouse designed by Sir Norman Foster; Professor Charles Stirton, the director of this garden among the Welsh hills, says that his intention is to display "the ideal planet" here, in a protected environment. Professor Stirton and Ivor Stokes (the head gardener and an eternal idealist) are clearly delighted with their translucent dome, which is 360 feet (110 meters) long, 200 feet (60 meters) wide, and made of 780 glass panels. In this astonishing flying saucer near Llanarthne,

fifteen gardeners have planted "Mediterranean" species from Europe, Chile, California, South Africa, and Australia. In a ravine 20 feet (6 meters) deep, visitors can walk among miniature cliffs and waterfalls, admiring trees from the Himalayas, the Andes, or Natal. A few years from now, nearly 12,000 different species will cohabit in this park. According to curator Wolfgang Bopp, the goal is to re-create different environments that will teach people to respect, and therefore protect, nature. They expect an estimated 250,000 visitors every year: when these people leave the park, they will have learned a lot about the mistakes of the past, and will be better prepared to take an active role in shaping a more ecologically responsible future.

Even more impressive is the world's biggest greenhouse, baptised "The Eden Project", which opened in early 2001, in a disused china clay quarry in Cornwall after seven years' planning. The 50 hectare (502,222 square meter) site, which cost £86 million, is home to structures called "biomes," made of high-tech galvanized steel coated with polymer foil. The largest building at the Eden Project, the Humid Tropics Biome, houses a variety of tropical plants in an area of 1.55 hectares (15,590 square meters). There is also a Warm Temperate Biome, about half as big. The biomes are home to a stunning variety of plants, although since this is a long-term research project, maximum plant coverage representing a fully developed ecosystem will not be achieved for

Thanks to the determination of the landscape gardener Albert Tourette, twenty or so Australian plants (of venerable age) were brought to Paris and have taken root in the greenhouses in the Parc André-Citroën, Paris (left and facing page).

fifteen years, with seedlings coming from all over the world. In the biomes, animals such as birds and geckoes will be used as pest control, in keeping with the desire for an entirely natural, non-polluting site (in the long run, all its systems will be powered by renewable energy, and all water on-site is recycled). The site runs a breeding program for endangered species, in particluar conifers, such as *Fitzroyia* from the Chilean Andes.

A similar project, though on a smaller scale, opened in 1992 in Montreal. The Biodôme shelters four different ecosystems, from the polar regions of the Far North to the tropical rainforest of Central America, from the great deciduous forests of

Theme gardens have replaced the former wine warehouses in the Bercy district of Paris. A Lloyd Loom armchair (above) in the setting of a modern conservatory adjoining the former customs house, now devoted to the art of gardening. It leads to a teaching greenhouse for schoolchildren.

Canada to the Saint Lawrence River estuary. Each of these ecosystems is a real laboratory for the scientists who work on the site, allowing them to study the impact of logging on forest soil or the behavior of bats in the wild, for example. The site has already welcomed over eight million visitors.

All of these modern greenhouses have one thing in common: a desire to pass on the vital message that mankind must interact positively with the environment if we are to survive. Our future depends just as much as it ever did on the natural world, and the dedicated botanists, ecologists and scientists behind these triumphs of engineering work constantly to preserve many threatened plants and animals. The Royal Botanic Garden at Kew, for instance, runs a breeding program for the endangered West African tree *Prunus Africana*, which could be a weapon in the fight against prostate cancer. Research and progress in the field of botany never ends: a species, *Dombeya mauritiana*, on the verge of extinction, was pulled back from the brink at Brest Conservatory in Brittany; the only survivor

of this species left in its native Mauritius was a male tree, whose pollen was useless as all the female specimens had died. Other male plants were produced from cuttings brought back to the Conservatory. The biologist Stéphane Buord then attempted and accomplished a miracle: hormone therapy turned a few male flowers into females! These new females were then pollinated by males, and the resulting seeds were sown, ensuring the survival of *Dombeya mauritiana*. According to

a report by the International Union for the Conservation of Nature, nearly 1,000 species of trees are currently in danger, so we may well see other "emergency greenhouses" like this developing in the near future.

Sir Norman Foster's space-age greenhouse (above) seems to hover over the Welsh countryside like something out of a novel by Jules Verne. The Victorian "People's Palace," however, clearly belongs to a bygone age (top).

The Conservatory: a Way of Life

T *he humble winter shelter became an orangery, the orangery evolved into a greenhouse—and the greenhouse inspired such enthusiasm over the years that it has come to symbolize a way of life. Now, after an eclipse of over fifty years (due as much to changing fashions as to the effects of two world wars), the greenhouse has emerged from its ashes once again and been adapted to the demands of modern life. And in this Internet age, its old-world charm is no doubt the secret of its success.*

A hedonist's haven

It is halfway between house and garden. It is an in-between place in which to while away an hour or two, enjoying the heady scents of the flowers. If you have ever tasted the pleasures of the conservatory, you will understand why it inspires so many dreams. Where else can one enjoy

the comfort of the house without being indoors, or the pleasures of the garden without going outside? Which other room adds such a poetic dimension to everyday life?

Some people have acquired a new house with a conservatory attached, and only then discovered its delights. It is the perfect place for creating an atmosphere worthy of one's passions. Mme. Carven (of the famous fashion house) has just such a passion for birds, and she transformed the conservatory at her country house in France into a temple in their honor. She invites her friends to tea there, under the attentive eye of a stuffed flamingo (the sole survivor, unfortunately, of a colony which was stolen over ten years ago by unscrupulous "bird lovers"). On the other side of the channel, in the English countryside, Lady Palumbo uses her conservatory to display her collection of beautiful antique cages. As it seemed a shame to leave such masterpieces empty, the conservatory was soon full of twitterings and chirpings, yet Lady Palumbo herself was rather taken aback by the attention all these winged tenants required. So now there are only a few, including a magnificent, brightly-colored macaw who is guest of honor at every brunch or lunch. The delighted owner explains that this new room was initially intended to transform the uncomfortable, windy terrace; but it soon turned out to be a more attractive place than the dining room itself. The overall effect is one of magic and mystery: the mirrors, which are cleverly placed to make the room look bigger, reflect a tumbling cascade of greenery, dotted with elegant bird cages and pretty cane furniture.

This greenhouse, formerly a total ruin, was renovated so successfully that it looks as though it has always belonged to the house. It is a lovely place to have tea, among the passion flowers, in the soft light of the garden. The roof of the greenhouse was designed by an English firm (page 100).
Designer Fabienne Villacrèces's favorite moments are those spent enjoying family lunches in the orangery of her seventeenth-century manor house, among the trimmed boxwood and lemon trees (above).
A wonderful example of Victorian architecture: the winter garden at Castle Leslie in Ireland, which used to receive many illustrious visitors, including royalty from all over the world. It has now been renovated and is open to the public; accommodation is available in the castle (facing page).

Dinner in

the conservatory

The conservatory (the "greenhouse within the house") is usually the ideal place to entertain friends: a meal in such a setting can be an unforgettable experience. Such buildings are not restricted to great country houses or to those with huge gardens: even in the city, many homes have their own small conservatory, hidden away unsuspected behind high railings in a little cul-de-sac. It can be the heart of the home and a haven of hospitality, in the center of the city, yet a million miles distant from the stresses and strains of city life. As night begins to fall over the city, in the flickering candlelight, dinner guests are charmed into another world.

As anyone who has tried it will confirm, eating in the conservatory is delightfully habit-forming. For Peter Marston, the well-known interior designer and creator (in 1972) of the English firm Marston & Langinger, it also reflects the importance attached to hospitality. In the introduction to his marvelous book on the subject, Marston admits that he cannot live in a house without a conservatory, and stresses the importance of its proximity to the kitchen. It is worth careful planning to ensure that the place where din-

A conservatory with typically Victorian charm, designed by decorator Nina Campbell and used as a beautiful extra room (facing page).
In the Cotentin region of France, a greenhouse full of orange trees, bougainvilleas, and geraniums (above).

ner is prepared is near to where it is served: this may be an apparently small detail, but it helps you and your guests appreciate life's little pleasures to the full.

Marston is a man of taste, who puts his theories into practice whenever he can—so his store in the heart of London is a delightful place. Every detail is charming: the furniture, antique tiling, statues, beautiful pieces of pottery, and all kinds of tableware are selected to demonstrate that entertaining is indeed an art.

The kitchen conservatory is the most convivial of places, designed with company in mind. It is a light, bright, and open place, which can inspire any cook to try out new recipes. But no detail must be overlooked; even more than in a classical kitchen,

In designer Andrée Putman's Parisian roof-garden, the plants grow outside the conservatory. In summer, many a starlit dinner takes place in this lovely setting (facing page and above). This conservatory is both dining room and comfortable living room: a house in itself (left).

simplicity and efficiency are the keywords. Transparency is a marvelous plus, provided it doesn't become a headache and draw attention to unnecessary clutter. Unsurprisingly, the interior designer Andrée Putman has created her own kitchen conservatory with good sense and taste. It is in the roof-garden of her Parisian apartment, and although it is not intended for plants, it is surrounded by them. There is a "nursery" for a small collection of orchids, which regain their strength here before flowering again. There are home-grown herbs, of course, as this is a place for cooking, and a place for enjoying food. A marble-topped table in the conservatory is ideal for breakfast, or for intimate lunches and dinners.

This Swedish dining room overlooking a fjord, with its white wood trim and large picture windows, looks ideal for a leisurely Sunday brunch (above). This simple but refined Marston & Langinger conservatory is a perfect example of how natural materials and daylight create a beautifully mellow effect (facing page).

Relaxing in the conservatory

Hugh Johnson, the famous British wine writer, dreamed of a room in which he could relax at any time of day. The large, bright conservatory at Hugh and Julia Johnson's home corresponds to this dream, and also gives them the pleasure of flowering plants all through the winter. Orange and lemon trees, and the delicate *Camellia sasanqua* with its iridescent pink flowers, can brighten the dullest November

day. Another lovely color combination: the purple tints of a *Salvia ambigens*, var. *caerulea*, the golden yellow of a mahonia, and the creamy white of *Acacia podalyriifolia*. Two electric radiators keep the winter temperature above 32°F (0°C), usually

In Hugh Johnson's house, the conservatory has become the family's favorite place. The sunlight filters through exterior cedar-wood blinds, creating a shady, romantic atmosphere (facing page). In a classical, rather dark apartment, opening a conservatory is a way of making the most of what light there is (above). Artists and architects often find that the light in a conservatory makes it an ideal place in which to work (left).

The English are experts at bringing
a conservatory to life; a lovely place
to come home to after a long walk
in the country (above).
In 1962, famous designer and
photographer Sir Cecil Beaton had
a conservatory added to his house
in Wiltshire. He used to fill it with
the flowers he grew in the next-door
greenhouse, and welcome his friends
there, in a décor of Chinese stools and
thoughtful mermaids (facing page).

nearer to 41°F (5°C), in which such tender plants thrive surprisingly well, and without which certain species (like *Leucaena leucocephala* with its pale yellow flowers and lovely ferny leaves) would not survive. Hugh Johnson loves to read the papers or just sit and relax in these pleasant surroundings. The conservatory is rarely empty: it is an ideal place for quiet times alone, or for sociable times with friends (when the terracotta statue of Bacchus looks particularly appropriate). Hugh Johnson is renowned for his works on wine, but also for his books and articles on gardening: he has opened Saling Hall (his property at Great Saling, near Braintree in Essex) to the public, and apart from the arboretum, the aquatic garden, and flower beds, the conservatory is a compulsory part of the visit.

The conservatory can easily become the family's favorite place. When designer Sonia Rykiel is not busy launching a collection of haute couture, she likes to relax in the cozy room she has created. This conservatory has no particular function, so it ends up being used for all kinds of things. It is the place where she eats, reads, writes, or plays cards. It is also a place where the family likes to gather at the first ray of sunshine, and it is the perfect place for small dinner parties (larger ones take place in the dining room).

Embroidered cushions are scattered here and there on the stylish antique sofas and cane furniture

that Sonia Rykiel found when treasure-hunting in Britain. There is a wrought-iron table with matching chairs, and large, warm-colored kilim rugs (inherited from her grandmother) brighten the natural tones of the floor. Huge tubs of hydrangeas and geraniums complete the picture—with a large bouquet of roses on the table to add the finishing touch.

This lovely Parisian conservatory is an example of what can be achieved with limited space (facing page).
In this conservatory in the south of France, the orange trees move out in the summer to make way for a dining room, illuminated with dozens of candles which shine their welcome into the night (right, top and bottom).

Conversions

Maybe you are lucky enough to own some kind of outbuilding for which you have no particular use: you don't need to extend your house, but it seems rather a shame to store a few garden tools and a wheelbarrow in such a big space. With a little imagination, you can convert it into something special.

A lovely example of this are Edith Wharton's greenhouses at her home The Mount, in Lenox, Massachusetts. The gardens at The Mount are especially important because it was the owner herself, a keen gardener, who designed them. Her niece, famous landscape gardener Beatrix Farrand, is known to have laid out the entrance drive and the kitchen garden, and other professionals contributed advice on plants and construction, but Edith Wharton planned and planted her own flower gardens. She was a knowledgeable horticulturist, having undertaken the study of botany years earlier, even as a young bride visiting Sicily and the Greek islands in 1888. She carefully planned her color palette and a sequence of blooming periods so the gardens were always in flower. Her gardens were much admired in their prime. Mrs. Daniel Chester French, for example, who often visited The Mount with her husband the sculptor, described the estate as "one of the most exquisite to be found anywhere in the Berkshires," with the view from its terrace "like an old tapestry." Today, restoration work has brought back the former glory of this beautiful site.

Roger Smith (who works in the American film industry) made a more radical conversion when he transformed several former greenhouses into a delightful home. This haven of greenery in the legendary Beverly Hills district of Los Angeles is half-house, half-garden: the original structures included the gardener's house (a small Tudor-style building from the 1920s) and greenhouses used for raising plants and cuttings. The result is a work of art,

For those who imagine that the conservatory is still a rather old-world place, here is Roger Smith's resolutely modern version. The white sofas and modern paintings create an elegant symmetry (facing page). Hanging paintings on the glass walls creates a more intimate atmosphere. Conservatories can also be created for dramatic effect, like this spectacular one in Saint-Tropez (right).
This conservatory in the heart of Nîmes is a wonderfully mysterious place, a perfect setting for a film by Visconti. Its varied collection of tropical plants can be admired from the patio, with its elegant antique furniture and colonnade (following double page).

dedicated to nature. Roger Smith wanted to respect the history of the place, so he made the transformation gradually, only changing what was necessary to allow him to live in comfort. There are plant motifs along the bedroom and bathroom walls, and the structure of the old roof has been kept (but it is now opaque, to reduce the effect of the strong summer sunshine). The furniture is varied, but bamboo and cane are favorites. The overall effect is soft and pleasant, with white walls and decorative green touches. Roger Smith says he draws his energy from the wonderful quality of light he enjoys all year round.

Two examples from the South of France:
On a hot day in Nîmes, when the cicadas are humming outside, an open book patiently awaits its reader's return (facing page).
In this huge house in Pézenas, even at the height of summer there is always a pleasant place in which to cool down with an iced drink, and admire the rich variety of plants (above).

The conservatory:
an extra room

If you want to build a veranda on a roof or small terrace in a city or town, you must respect the immediate environment and comply with local legislation regarding buildings that face each other. A conservatory in the garden usually gives one greater freedom. The first, crucial decision is whether to build it onto the house itself or make it a separate building. There will be personal considerations (perhaps you want to add a room to your house, or maybe your idea is to create a little, independent house), and there are practical elements to take into account. One advantage of extending an existing room is that the inner room will be much better insulated, even if the conservatory itself is not heated. A pale December sun can quickly warm the atmosphere in the conservatory, and therefore in the adjoining room too. One disadvantage is a loss of light on sunny days, when the blinds are down in the conservatory to keep it cool. This may seem like a minor inconvenience, however, especially as the summer months are also those that are spent outside or in the conservatory, when a little shade indoors tends to be welcome.

A conservatory separate from the house offers a completely different experience. Heating costs may be higher (although this depends on how much time you intend to spend there, and for what

Most houses (and even apartments) can be extended by a glass extension which will make an ideal conservatory (left). It can transform a Parisian courtyard planted with hydrangeas (facing page).
In this house in the suburbs of Amsterdam, the glass panels of the conservatory can be removed, so that on hot summer days there is no longer a barrier between indoors and outdoors (following double page).

purpose), but there is no doubt that stepping inside your little glass house is like entering another world, with its own special atmosphere and its own décor.

Whether it is part of the house or not, a conservatory should ideally face southwest (or west). The orangeries of the past all faced due south, since it was essential for them to maintain a temperature above 32°F (0°C) in winter, but specialists now agree that southwest (or west) is preferable. If your conservatory faces due south, the heat can quickly become unbearable in the summer, and many plants suffer from too much sunlight through the glass all day—while if it faces north, few plants will thrive, although, with adequate heating and insulation, it could be ideal for an office or studio, perfect for an architect or someone who works from home.

Even on a small terrace, you can build a little conservatory from which you can enjoy a view of the surrounding rooftops all year round (above). In the great Victorian tradition, this house seems to be attached to its park by the addition of a conservatory (right).
A conservatory can also be used to link two buildings; with a glass roof and a façade which opens onto the garden, an extra room is created (bottom of facing page). Modest or magnificent, it will be especially appreciated if it leads straight to the garden (top of facing page).

A place for plants or for people?

Victorian conservatories were designed to house splendid plant collections; nowadays, the conservatory seems to be designed with people in mind, but this does not mean that today's garden-lovers have sacrificed their passion or locked their planters away. Every month, firms specializing in greenhouse construction receive orders from serious gardeners for buildings great and small, with special shelves for seedlings or cuttings,

exclusively intended for growing plants. One of the gardener's greatest joys is to witness the miracle of the seed that sprouts, when a light spray of mist from the watering system or watering-can moistens the air and awakens the sleeping plant within. Lifting the protective netting is like peeping into an incubator, while sowing seeds is an almost magical experience. It is a privilege and a joy to see seeds that look like particles of dust sprouting, developing, and

flowering, producing the most magnificent, colored and scented blooms. Many people like to specialize in one sort of plant, whether it be delicate Japanese bonsaï that bear tiny, edible fruit, or fleshy, sensual cactus plants, or lacy ferns. Others create a special garden environment to attract butterflies or bees, others still a haven of strongly-scented plants for the visually impaired. Some gardeners are so proud of their efforts that they open their home to visitors and fellow garden lovers. In Great Britain, the National Gardens Scheme runs a program every summer of such gardens open to the public, with the proceeds going to charity.

So what do you think? Is the conservatory for cultivating plants or friendships? In any case, if you're the kind of person who has always enjoyed "messing about in the garden," you can be sure that once you have your greenhouse, only an earthquake will get you out of it.

A lovely little greenhouse for plants only, but one can imagine a litle frog hopping in to cool down on a warm July evening (above). A place in which to enjoy the art of repotting.
According to Hugh Johnson, the height of luxury is a greenhouse-annex for growing tropical plants to brighten your conservatory all year round (facing page).
Miniature greenhouses are much sought-after for their old-world charm. One can buy them in specialist stores for cultivating rare plants (following double page).

Whatever their function, the beauty of certain greenhouses seems to justify their existence. On a sunny day, such places are as awe-inspiring as silent, glass cathedrals, in which the visitor is completely captivated by the magic of the present moment. One such greenhouse can be found among the greenery in the park of the Château de Roussan. The house itself is now a hotel, whose guests can admire a lovely (recently restored) nineteenth-century greenhouse. In the metal framework, which rests on low, sculpted stone walls, the narrow glass panels reflect the glorious southern sunshine. It is the kind of place that lingers on in the memory, alive with the promise of future flowers.

The greenhouse sometimes seems to inspire its owners with a generosity born of a shared passion. Recently, for example, a keen orchid grower gave a collection of over eight hundred orchids to

Yves Saint Laurent president Pierre Bergé's greenhouse in Saint-Rémy-de-Provence fits in perfectly among the boxwood and olive trees (above). In southern France, the greenhouse is an ideal refuge when the mistral is blowing, and can shelter tender plants like the plumbago.
This model is a perfect replica of the cloche our grandparents used (right), but lighter, being made of translucent, recycled plastic.
The watering-can in this well-kept greenhouse is just posing for the photo. It will soon be off on its rounds again (facing page).

The glazed earthenware, old zinc watering-cans, and other well-worn gardening tools, together with the foliage and bright-colored pumpkins in this old orangery, create a romantic atmosphere (left).
The greenhouses in the Château de la Bourdaisière on the banks of the Loire river are a must for visitors (facing page).

the New York Botanical Garden. He and his wife had been growing these delicate and much-loved flowers for over fifty years, and decided to share their magnificent collection with others. You may not have such a fine collection of rare breeds and hybrids in your greenhouse, but friends and neighbors will surely appreciate a bouquet of home-grown flowers or a bunch of grapes in December.

In colder climates, those lucky enough to be planning a swimming pool may wish to install it in the greenhouse, rather than under the open sky. Imagine the luxury of gazing up at a rainy or snowy sky from the warmth of the water! How wonderful to float on your back and watch the birds fly over! In a greenhouse aquarium, the choice of colors is all-important to provide extra warmth. You can create an impression of calm and serenity with soft tones that match the tiles or bricks, for example, and the armchairs you have chosen to relax in after your swim will look especially inviting. Moreover, plants love this warm, humid atmosphere, and they should be given pride of place.

A swim is even more delightful
with luxuriant ferns overhanging
the pool, but because
of the chlorinated atmosphere,
the owner of this astonishing
greenhouse (a Buenos Aires
antique-dealer) grows them
in huge pots. One can tell the
owner is a collector from the
precious objects dotted among
the orchids in this hot, humid
atmosphere.

Greenhouse designers

Greenhouse construction techniques nowadays benefit from all the latest technology in terms of materials and design, while keeping sight of the traditions that have stood the test of time. So why not treat yourself to the luxury of your own "glass house"? It can be whatever you want it to be: office, studio, kitchen, bathroom, dining room, or living room—whatever it is, the plants will provide a link between your indoor and outdoor worlds. In any case, you should ask for advice before getting started (which any manufacturer will be happy to provide). Have several plans drawn up before you finalize things. Don't be afraid to use your imagination—but don't forget that the structural harmony of your home is at stake. There is a greenhouse to suit every kind of house, so beware of choosing something that looks great in a catalogue but would be totally inappropriate in view of your own house's style, volume, and surroundings. Try not to think too big. A large space is harder to heat, and more difficult to equip. If you're thinking of an office or bathroom, you won't need the space required by a family dining room or living room. In other words, think in terms of elegance and moderation rather than grandeur and excess. Plan things carefully to avoid future disappointments.

No matter how large or small your property, go over it in detail, armed with your plans, and try to envisage the completed project. Do you like it? Or do the designer's sketches need modifying here and there? You need professional advice, of course, but you also need to follow your dreams. Any manufacturer worthy of his profession will be keen to hear your view of things, to ensure that his construction will correspond to your own ideas.

Understanding what the customer wants is the first step to producing something that comes as close as possible to his dream. A deciding factor, obviously, is the financial one; but this should not prevent you from telling the architect or planner exactly what you wish to see take shape. You will soon be able to define the kind of greenhouse you want, and the kind of greenhouse you can afford. Talk to friends, too, and go to professional exhibitions to find the manufacturer who will suit you best and be most sensitive to your taste. Why not combine business with pleasure, by visiting places that have already been restored or created by the firm you've contacted? Many firms sprang up in the 1980s, but only those that can guarantee quality have survived.

The English firm Amdega designed this conservatory (above), which links house and garden. It is a pleasant place at any time of day, but looks quite magical at night; a wonderful place to unwind after a busy day. Roger Hager, a greenhouse manufacturer based in the Paris region, is famous for his restoration work, but he also likes to create little summerhouses for public or private gardens. Here are some examples of his work, from the most humble to the most sophisticated (facing page).

English firms like Amdega and Marston & Langinger, which keep a certain tradition alive and are an inspiration to lesser-known manufacturers, are also worthy of interest. To sum up, make the most of this preparatory phase, take your time, let your plans take shape—and the chances are you will not be disappointed.

Luc d'Hulst, who is based near Antwerp, is one of the best-known conservatory designers around today. His career began with a drawing: a friend asked him to do a sketch of the greenhouse he planned to build, and a passion was born. Now this eclectic designer creates glass cathedrals for the green-thumbed, all over the world. He never tires of exploring the seemingly infinite possibilities of glass, of experimenting with its transparency, allying it with the strength of steel and titanium. Each project is an entirely new experience, but his aim is always harmony of structure: sometimes it is an extension to a house, sometimes a roof over a terrace, sometimes a shed which opens up to the sky, but every new job is a fresh challenge. He draws, listens, explains, and finally entrusts his team with the actual construction. In his personal paradise at Zandhoven, Belgium, he is free to experiment with lifestyles, and as his mood changes, so does his house! It may suddenly grow glass wings, for example, which turn into a study or a kitchen. He finds that living under glass is a constant source of inspiration and balance. It is also the best way of

Panes of glass in delicate cedar-wood or metal frames: these English conservatories (facing page) were inspired by antique models and made to order for the customer. Their owners can use the terrace all year round. By adding a conservatory, one can enjoy extra light on a gray and cloudy day. It is a real "room with a view," which helps to make the most of a lovely garden.
Above top: A creation by the famous London firm Marston & Langinger.
Above bottom: A conservatory by Vale Garden Houses Ltd., a firm based in Lincolnshire which specializes in old-style conservatories, from the Gothic to the Victorian.

communing with nature, either as an admiring onlooker or an active participant (when caring for the tender species that need help to survive the winter). So how should we describe this glass house, in which plants flower all year round? Is it an extension to the house, encroaching on the garden—or a a clever and beautiful way of welcoming Nature indoors?

Luc d'Hulst, past master of glass architecture, is based in the heart of the Flemish countryside. For him, the garden is not simply "a fragment of countryside, composed outside the house—but an oasis of greenery including the house itself, which seems to spread its light transparent wings." Are his conservatories extensions of the garden or of the house? Here are three examples to help you decide (above and facing page).

Material matters

Once you have decided where to build your greenhouse, you must choose your materials. Technical progress has made it possible to use inexpensive materials like aluminum (although some manufacturers dislike it for aesthetic reasons). It is worth knowing, however, that apart from being stainless, it can provide perfect insulation for a greenhouse. Iron is still the favorite, however, and current techniques, such as plating by covering it with pure zinc at 840°F (450°C), ensure protection against corrosion. If your conservatory is treated this way, it will not require any more attention for another twenty years, and there will be no sign of rust for another forty years at least!

Another favorite material is wood, which has always been preferred to metal when constructing English-style greenhouses for fruit and vegetables. It is also very efficient in the winter for keeping warmth inside the greenhouse. Provided it is guaranteed rot-proof (either naturally or after some

appropriate treatment), it will stand up to all weathers. Several exotic woods can be used: for example, the Traditional English Conservatory Company uses mahogany from West Africa. Other builders prefer red cedar or teak. However, many people prefer to use wood that is guaranteed to come from properly farmed, sustainable woodland resources. You may wish to ask the company you are working with to check this before beginning. Some companies, such as Arbor Vetum in Petersfield, Hampshire, even use recycled teak in their creations.

Whatever wood you choose, you should never use varnish: don't forget that wood is a living material that needs to breathe. Aluminum has the considerable advantage of reducing maintenance costs, but it looks lighter and less elegant than wood or iron. So study your estimates in detail: aesthetics come at some cost, and if you dream of a Victorian-style conservatory, it would be a shame if the result is not up to your expectations.

So much progress has been made that it is now perfectly feasible to live under glass all year round, and all kinds of possibilities can be envisaged.

The tall glass panes of this private greenhouse in Holland are reflected in the pool, accentuating the impression of fusion between the house and nature. Its high gable creates a grandiose effect at the entrance to the house (above). Another high gable, in a greenhouse designed by the English decorator John Stefanidis, with wooden rather than metal uprights, and a brick floor (facing page). It creates a very high room, in contrast with the low rooms of the adjoining house.

The owner of a rather dark house in London's Hampstead area, for example, wanted to brighten it up by adding a large transparent structure to the roof, with a living room underneath.

An architect friend designed this modern "winter garden," taking advantage of all the latest technological improvements. With treble-thickness glass (parts of which conduct heat) there is no longer any risk that your beautiful construction will be uncomfortably cold. And as for privacy: at the press of a button, the glass becomes opaque! No danger of being spied on! Loft-dwellers can also use this "adaptable" glass, when they don't want to be "on show."

The manufacturer will help you choose—smash-proof laminated glass, double or triple glazing?—according to the site of your conservatory and the local climate (some reflective glass acts like a filter and is recommended in very sunny areas). As a general rule, small panes may look charming, but larger ones reduce the number of joints and consequently the risk of infiltration due to the accumulation of dirt, the growth of moss, and so on. Any serious specialist will also use discreet anti-corrosive fastenings, usually made of copper. And finally: plastic gutters are not a good idea! Apart from their appearance, they may not stay firm when you lean your ladder against them! A rigid metal is preferable.

The framework of your building will rest on a stone or brick base: if your conservatory is to look Victorian, you'll no doubt prefer brick. The floor itself needs to be both practical and aesthetic: the main thing is to respect the style of the rest of the building. Peter Marston stresses the importance of harmonizing the various materials around the fundamental element: the floor. By hunting in markets or architectural salvage yards, you can often find the most attractive old materials, but beware! A floor worthy of a banqueting hall may look out of place. Aim for discretion: a conservatory floor should look as natural as possible. Stone, tiles, brick, or baked earthenware are perfect.

An indoor garden is a place for sitting, relaxing, reading, drinking tea, and chatting, whatever the weather (above). But it is not always easy to decide where to build the conservatory so that it fits perfectly into the garden. It is a good idea, especially in sunny areas, to build it near trees that will shade it from the summer sunshine (facing page).

When a veranda adjoins another room. you can unify the two by using the same flooring. When you want to make the place look more cozy. you can put down large. comfortable rugs. which will also come in useful to cheer up dull December days. Remember. though. that the temperature can vary and that the atmosphere is humid: your rugs cannot be a permanent feature. It is perhaps wiser to use natural materials. such as sisal. jute. coconut fiber or seagrass. The best flooring in any case is a resistant material unaffected by temperature changes—and which lets you open the doors wide and wash the floor down if required (a gentle slope will make this easier).

A question of atmosphere . . .

Light, shade, heating, ventilation, and humidity: these are key words in the greenhouse-owner's vocabulary. And don't suppose that they are only of interest to plant fanatics; your greenhouse is essentially a "glass house," and even if it is an integral part of your home, it is more exposed to changes in weather than the rest of the building. If you suffocate there in summer or freeze to death in winter, you won't want to spend much time in it. The evolution of the greenhouse has taught us that plants and humans require the same kind of care and conditions if they are to thrive and be happy. Plants need light to grow, but they also need air; your greenhouse must therefore be well-ventilated, especially as the temperature inside can reach 120°F (50°C) on hot summer days. You will have to plan the ventilation system well in advance, for it is difficult to incorporate one as an afterthought. To keep the air circulating regularly, it is recommended to equip the greenhouse with openings that correspond to twenty percent of the surface area of glass. Apart from the doors and windows,

there can be openings in the upper part of the greenhouse, and grids in the stone or brick base. You can also have a slow-turning fan on the ceiling. Considerable improvements have been made over the last few years, and most major manufacturers suggest automatic ventilation and shutter systems, activated by heat and rainfall.

The crucial question of heating depends on how you intend to use your conservatory. Will it be a living room, or a place for growing rare orchids? In these cases, you will need an elaborate system of radiators or underfloor heating. But if you just want to make sure it doesn't freeze inside, a couple of gas or electric heaters will be enough. Be sure to evaluate your needs realistically from the start. Heating can be very costly, especially as a lot of heat is lost through glass. A conservatory that adjoins another room will be heated via the latter's heating system, but it will need a separate thermostat to compensate for the drop in temperature during the coldest nights of the year, when you may have turned the heating down in the rest of your house.

Whatever the weather outside, if your conservatory is a warm and pleasant place it can easily

All owners of conservatories agree that ventilation is very important, to avoid creating a "furnace" in summer. The shade provided by a vine in a conservatory is an attractive alternative to a blind (above). One of the joys of the greenhouse has always been the luxury of fruit in the middle of winter, such as oranges, lemons, pineapples, and grapes: Muscat from Hamburg or Alexandria, and succulent Chasselas from Fontainebleau (facing page).

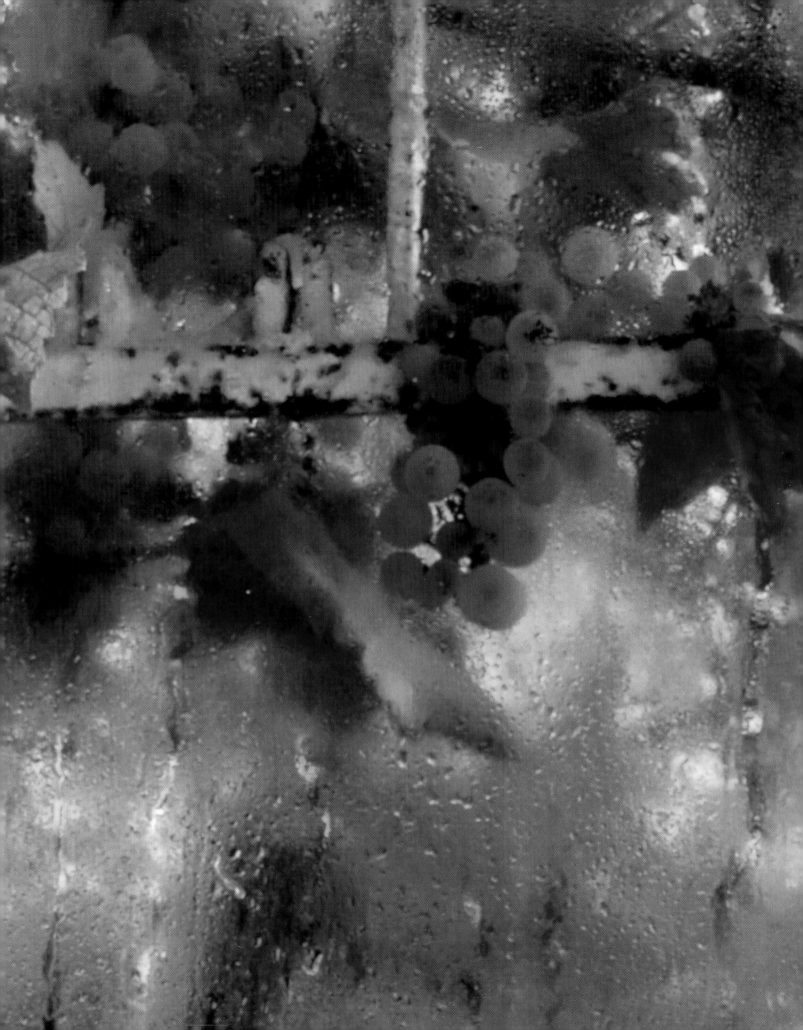

become the most attractive part of the house. Greenery, color, and warmth are very enticing on a cold, wet day. In Howard Hawks's legendary film *The Big Sleep* (1946) starring Humphrey Bogart and Lauren Bacall, the father of the Bacall character is a grumpy old soldier, who has turned his conservatory into a sort of headquarters—such a comfortable place that he hardly ever leaves it. Alone in his humid domain, surrounded by his rare plants, he is furious with anyone else who dares to enter. This is proof, once again, that there is no typical conservatory, and that yours will gradually become a place that reflects your moods.

A pleasant atmosphere depends on good ventilation, but there is also the question of shade. Exterior wooden blinds were the favorites for a long time, because they kept the sun off the glass but did not hinder the growth of climbing plants on the inside. Over the years, wood has sometimes been replaced by (treated) plaited straw, but some manufacturers still prefer wood, and now use treated fir for trellis blinds. However, there is obviously a wider selection of attractive interior blinds, or even curtains, as they are not exposed to the elements. You may find that the foliage above your conservatory provides sufficient shade: yuccas, palm trees,

or araucarias can be particularly efficient and sun-resistant screens. However, you may opt for a solution that is both efficient and romantic: an indoor vine, which will provide refreshing shade from springtime through fall.

The watering system you choose will depend on the requirements of your plants. If your conservatory looks like a furnished living room with only a few decorative plants here and there, obviously it will not need as much water as a greenhouse for tropical or subtropical species. Once again, there are many possibilities, ranging from the traditional watering-can (undoubtedly the most efficient, but

time-consuming if you have a large plant collection) to automatic systems, which are obviously easier to use, and work even while you are away on holiday if you pre-program them; however, they are pricier than other methods. As for day-to-day air humidity, you can set misting systems to function at fixed times, to make sure your plants thrive in the best possible conditions; your work will be easier and the results better if you group them according to their need for watering and humidity. In most cases, a hand-held spray will be quite sufficient. Again, if your greenhouse looks more like a cozy living room than a clinic for botanical experiments, a collection of Mediterranean plants will be less work than more demanding tropical species, or plants that are known to be difficult, such as orchids (although some people have an almost magic affinity with orchids, successfully breeding them with very little effort). Otherwise, make sure you have a sink in a corner of your greenhouse.

In the early nineteenth century, the fashion was for "forcing houses" (facing page). In *Northanger Abbey*, Jane Austen mentions the hundreds of pineapples that were grown this way. Honoré de Balzac also cultivated them in his Parisian garden. In the open air, the gardener's responsibility is relative, but in the greenhouse it is total: water, earth, and light no longer depend on nature but on the gardener himself. Here, the protective blinds are outside the greenhouse, to filter the sun's rays before they reach the glass and burn the plants (above).

You can either hide this workplace behind a pretty screen of some kind or turn it into a feature of the place, if you can find an old sink and taps with a little character.

If you want to grow large plants in your greenhouse, you should reserve some open plots of earth for them; a weeping fig (*Ficus benjamina*) or an impressive *Philodendron* "Santa Leopoldina" (whose two-tone leaves can be up to a meter long) will be happy there. With a border of small bricks, these square or rectangular plots can be very attractive features. Another attractive option for larger plants is the Versailles-style planter—a large wooden crate used in the French château for bringing the king's collection of fig-trees indoors for the winter. You can also choose from an infinite variety of pots or bowls in which to test your new (or confirmed) gardening skills. Choose whatever shape you like, but please don't go for plastic—it is always ugly, especially when made to look like imitation terracotta, and is not really solid enough to resist any unexpected frost or shocks. Finally, to grow plants of different heights, try putting up shelves along one or more sides of your

greenhouse. Add a nineteenth-century wrought-iron plant stand (which you can find at a flea market), mingle several plants (ferns, begonias, and various species of *Columnea* or hanging fuchsia), and the effect will be charmingly Victorian. Nowadays, there are many antique dealers specializing in both decorative and functional garden furniture. and the only difficulty is in choosing which style to go for!

In Howard Hawks's film *The Big Sleep*, detective Philip Marlowe (played by Humphrey Bogart) is employed by an old general who lives among the orchids in a conservatory, and seems to thrive on the heat just as they do (facing page). When the conservatory is not overcrowded with plants, but is a place from which to admire the garden, interior fabric blinds filter the light, creating a comfortable setting in summer (above).

Choosing your furniture

Conservatory furniture is traditionally made of bamboo or cane. Apart from its resistance to humidity and temperature changes, it fits in perfectly with the glass and metal structure of the greenhouse and looks good with more recent wrought-iron furniture. As a natural product, its use in the greenhouse is particularly appropriate, especially when allied with natural floor coverings like jute or sisal. Its delicate tones create a soft, welcoming atmosphere whatever the time of day, whatever the weather outside. In the late nineteenth century, when the bourgeoisie began to add conservatories their houses, they wanted light, easy-to-handle furniture, which would be sufficiently comfortable and elegant to fit in with the furniture in the Napoleon III style which was in vogue at the time. As a taste for the exotic developed, bamboo or cane furniture was imported from Asia, and was gradually copied and adapted by European manufacturers. At first, they used imported cane or bamboo, but from the mid-nineteenth century onward the necessary plants were cultivated in mainland Europe. By hunting in markets and secondhand stores, you're sure to find examples of such treasures as Victorian plant-stands, work-tables, becnhes, seedling trays and shelves. Certain more intricate designs are few and far between, and fetch high prices at auction, but it is still relatively easy to find chaises longues or chairs from the 1930s at reasonable prices. Among the most sought-after of garden furniture items are Lloyd Loom armchairs. These first appeared in 1922; they were of neither cane nor bamboo, but of wire, wrapped in cleverly plaited brown wrapping paper. This revolutionary design was invented by Marshall Burns Lloyd in 1917. The new loom-woven fabric meant that a Lloyd Loom Chair could be produced in a quarter of the time it took to make a rattan or wicker version. The end product was not only cheaper but much more durable, and soon appeared in stately or more modest homes, restaurants, hotels, and on the decks of ocean-going liners. It even graced the Royal Boxes at Wimbledon, Henley and Twickenham. Today, furniture in this style is available in both the United States and Great Britain, although authentic pieces of original Lloyd Loom furniture from the 1920s is quickly snapped up by collectors.

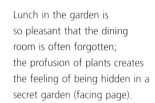

Wrought-iron furniture looks perfect in a conservatory; natural materials also look good and add a comfortable touch (right).

Lunch in the garden is so pleasant that the dining room is often forgotten; the profusion of plants creates the feeling of being hidden in a secret garden (facing page).

Specialized antiques fairs exist for the enthusiast, like the Antique Garden Furniture Show, held annually at the New York Botanic Gardens. Companies come from all over North America to display their treasures—all guaranteed genuine antiques—at this popular event.

Especially popular is cast-iron, marble or stone furniture such as benches. These bring a touch of romanticism to the greenhouse, and are often as decorative as they are functional. They are extremely heavy, so before investing make sure that the floor of your greenhouse will support the weight of your purchase. You may also like to add a few cushions to take off the chill and to ease your weary limbs after a hard day's gardening!

Cane and wicker furniture became popular when conservatories first came into fashion. Light, practical furniture was needed, which would also look comfortable and elegant in this new setting. The golden age of cane and bamboo lasted until the 1930s, but they have been back in fashion since the 1960s (above and facing page).

MEUBLES DE JARDIN
CHAISES LONGUES EN OSIER

As a general rule, it is best to choose conservatory furniture in natural materials and colors, as it will harmonize with the view outside (be it park, garden, or simply sky). If you add a pretty table-cloth, some old lanterns and a chipped pedestal table with one or two secondhand pitchers, your conservatory will look so comfortable and attractive that it will soon be the family's favorite place.

Whether you go there to read quietly for an hour or two, to enjoy a romantic meal, to host a large dinner party, or even, as in times past, to propose on one knee to your beloved, you'll find that your conservatory can suit all kinds of moods, all kinds of occasions. At different times of year, you can watch the clouds float by, or just spend a peaceful moment alone . . . and you'll understand exactly why so many other gardeners, artists, and poets have already treated themselves to the luxury of such a haven, in which dallying the time away becomes a fine art. At any time of night or day, in any kind of weather, you will always be sure of a warm welcome in your glass sanctuary.

A lean-to veranda created by Peter Marston for his London house. For a completely harmonious effect, the wooden trim is pale green, the wooden blinds are dark green, and the table-top is made of green gypsum (following page).

These inviting wicker chaises longues featured in the 1900 catalogue of the Saint-Etienne munitions and bicycle factory (above). Old models are much sought-after by collectors (facing page, above, and right).

Address Book

Greenhouses to visit
Botanic Gardens and Private Parks

In a world where uncharted territory has become a thing of the past, greenhouses have often replaced distant lands as places worthy of discovery and exploration. The following list, although inevitably selective, features both public venues and lesser-known private gardens. These contain a wealth of secrets waiting to be discovered by anyone sensitive to the special atmosphere of greenhouses and the plants which thrive in them. Many of the greenhouses featured in these pages are also testaments to the passion and enthusiasm of the creators of these steel and glass creations, visionary architects pursuing the dream of transparency and light combined with nurturing strength to protect the tender plants within.

In the second part of this section, greenhouse enthusiasts will find a list of addresses providing a starting point to help them create the conservatory of their dreams.

United States

Atlanta Botanical Garden
1345 Piedmont Avenue
Atlanta, GA 30309
Tel.: 404 876-5859
www.atlantabotanicalgarden.org
Dedicated to research, the relatively recent (1989) construction of the greenhouse has given the botanic garden a focal point and a suitable setting for its exhibitions. The Dorothy Chapman Fuqua Conservatory is contemporary in style and houses a range of rare and endangered plants. The latest addition to the gardens is the orchid complex with the latest technology in climate control.

Brooklyn Botanic Garden
1000 Washington Ave,
Brooklyn, NY 11225
Tel.: 718 623-7200
www.bbg.org
Home to the recently constructed modern Steinhardt Conservatory, which incorporates a Palm House and an impressive Aquatic House.

Callaway Gardens
US Highway 27
Pine Mountain, GA 31822
Tel.: 706 663-2281
www.callawaygardens.com
The largest glass-enclosed tropical butterfly conservatory in North America is at Callaway Gardens in Pine Mountain. The Cecil B. Day Butterfly Center, which opened in September 1988, joins the ranks of the world's foremost butterfly conservatories in London, Melbourne, and Tokyo. Guests walk among plants and butterflies native to countries in Central and South America, Malaysia, Taiwan, and Africa.

The Climatron
Missouri Botanical Gardens
PO Box 299
Saint Louis, MI 63166-0299
Tel.: 314 577-5100
www.mobot.org
This stunning, geodesic-domed conservatory houses a tropical rainforest display, including streams, waterfalls, and some 1,200 species of plants in a natural setting, among them banana, cacao and coffee trees, lianas, bromeliads, cycads, passion flowers, and colorful orchids. Its shape was inspired by the futuristic design of R. Buckminster Fuller.

Como Park Conservatory
Como Park, St. Paul,
Minneapolis, MN 55130
Tel.: 615 487-8200
Erected by the King Construction Co. and Frederick Nussbaumer in 1915 and fully restored in 1983, the strengthened structure is a combination of aluminum, steel, and glass. In 1998, a sophisticated water management system was added to the conservatory. Como Park also contains a zoo which, in conjunction with the conservatory, holds an annual conference.

Druid Hill Park
Gwynns Fall Parkway and McCulloch Street, Baltimore MD 21209
Tel.: 410 396-0180
This estate inspired by an English garden and containing a manor house was bought by Baltimore Park Commission in 1860. The park is home to a number of buildings, notably the greenhouse known locally as the Palm House, which dates back to 1888 and contains a collection of tropical plants.

Dorrance H. Hamilton Fernery
100, Northwestern Avenue
Philadelphia, PA 19118
www.upenn.edu/morris/
This elegant, small glasshouse devoted entirely to ferns is a Victorian gem, unique in North America. Among its special features are a formal rose garden and rock wall garden. All in all, a charming site that reflects the Victorian spirit of its founders, John and Lydia Morris.

Edith Wharton's Greenhouse
EWR at The Mount
2 Plunkett Street, P.O. Box 974, Lenox Massachusetts 01240-0974
Tel 413 637 1899
Funded by the "Save America's Treasures" Trust, the Edith Wharton Restoration Project was completed in time for memorial day 2001. The novelist's Berkshire estate comprising her house

"The Mount" along with its gardens and greenhouse has been fully restored and will no doubt become a popular tourist attraction. The greenhouse, which dates back to 1902, was designed by Hitchings and Company and was used to cultivate seedlings—annuals and perennials—which Wharton later planted in her 150-acre gardens.

Golden Gate Park
John F. Kennedy Drive
San Francisco, CA 94117
Tel.: 415 666-7017
www.frp.org
Home to the Conservatory of Flowers, the oldest wooden glasshouse in the United States was constructed by the famed Frederick A. Lord in the 1870s. After it was partially destroyed by fire in 1883, it was redesigned in a highly ornate Victorian style. Currently being restored again in keeping with the 1890 design, it holds an impressive collection of plants, notably a 100-year-old philodendron and other rare species.

Irwin M. Krohn Conservatory
1501 Eden Park Drive
Cincinnati, OH 45202
Tel.: 513 421-5707
www.cinciparks.org
Dating from the 1930s, this conservatory displays a strong Art Deco influence, for example in its floral motifs and colorful stained-glass windows. It is located within Eden Park, which has been home to municipal greenhouses since the 1880s. Created by the architects Rapp and Meachem and taking its name from the park's commissioner, the conservatory is well maintained and boasts a selection of tropical plants and an impressive orchid display.

Lincoln Park
2400 N. Stockton Drive
Chicago, IL 60614
Tel.: 312 742-7736
Opened just prior to the great World's Columbian Exposition of 1893, both this park and Garfield Park (1908) are popular landmarks in Chicago. When it opened, Lincoln Park Conservatory was hailed as an innovative architectural triumph. Its showhouse holds five seasonal exhibitions a year.

The Lockwood-Mathews Mansion Museum
295 West Ave
Norwalk, CT 06850
Tel.: 203 838-9799
www.lockwoodmathews.org
A delightful little museum which is home to a charming conservatory converted into a tea shop.

Longwood Greenhouses
PO Box 501
Kennett Square, PA 19348-0501
Tel.: 610 388-1000
www.longwood gardens.org
This group of greenhouses houses no fewer than twenty different gardens and approximately 4,500 plant varieties. A charming walkway leads the visitor through an orangery, a camellia garden, the azalea house, a Mediterranean garden, and a tropical cascade garden, as well as a greenhouse devoted entirely to carnivorous plants.

Mitchell Park Conservatory
524 South Layton Boulevard
Milwaukee, WI 532155
Tel.: 414 649-9830
www.countyparks.com/horticulture
When the site's first conservatory was demolished following years of neglect, it was replaced by three unique "space age" greenhouses in 1955. The beehive-shaped domes are the work of architect Donald Grieb. Two domes exhibit permanent displays, whilst the third changes several times a year for shows. Together they hold thousands of species of plants as well as birds, turtles, frogs, and other creatures.

Moody Gardens
1 Hope Boulevard
Galveston, TX 77554
Tel.: 800 582-4673
Step inside a ten-story glass pyramid. Experience the rainforests of Africa, Asia, and the Americas. This site houses a full acre of natural wonders, from waterfalls, cliffs, caverns, to forests, and there is even a Mayan colonnade. The 250 square-foot, completely enclosed exhibit is also home to 60 Old and New World fruit bats native to Africa and South America.

The New York Botanical Garden
Bronx, New York 10458-5126
Tel.: 718 817-8616
Home to the most remarkable ensemble of Victorian greenhouses on American soil. The most noteworthy is the fully restored Enid A. Haupt Conservatory (built 1900) which is now an official New York City landmark. Showcasing plants from all of the main climatic regions, it was renovated in 1997. Its permanent collections as well as its temporary exhibitions attract thousands of visitors every year.

Rockwood Museum Conservatory
610 Shipley Road
Wilmington, DE 19809
Tel.: 302 761-4340
After falling in love with the English countryside, an American banker decided to build a Gothic-style manor on his return home, complete with a spectacular conservatory. Despite the harsh Delaware winters he was able contemplate his citrus fruits, gardenias, and a diverse selection of orchids at his leisure.

The U.S. Botanic Garden
245 First Street SW
Washington DC 20024
Tel.: 202 225-8333
www.aoc.gov
The idea of a national garden came from George Washington, but took more than a century to implement. Nevertheless, this is the oldest botanic garden in North America. Its first greenhouse was opened in 1842 while the current conservatory, opened in 1933, was built by Lord Burnham. After undergoing restoration

work, the conservatory was reopened in 2000. It hosts four annual flower shows exhibiting exotic plants and flowers from around the world. The Palm House and rare and endangered species house are also of interest.

England

Alton Towers Gardens
Staffordshire
Tel.: 01870 520 4060
Alton Towers is home to some of England's most beautiful historic gardens as well as Britain's best-known theme park. Former ancestral home of the Earls of Shrewsbury, the gardens were first landscaped in the early 1800s and purchased by a group of businessmen in 1924, who opened them to the public. With stunning conservatories and an unusual pagoda fountain, visitors can stroll through the gardens at their leisure or, if they prefer, contemplate them from above during the thrilling Sky Ride.

Athelhampton House and Gardens
Dorchester DT2 7LG
Tel.: 01305 848 363
Web: http://www.athelhampton.co.uk
Athelhampton is one of the finest fifteenth-century houses in England. The Great Hall was built by Sir William Martyn in 1485. The glorious Grade 1 gardens, dating from 1891, are full of vistas and include the world-famous topiary pyramids and two garden pavilions designed by Inigo Thomas. Fine collections of tulips, magnolias, roses, clematis, and lilies can also be seen in season.

Bicton Park
Budleigh Salterton
Devonshire
Tel.: 01345 568 465
Built at the beginning of the nineteenth century, the palm house at Bicton Park was one of the first of its kind. Undoubtedly the work of Loudon, its light and airy appearance makes it a particularly remarkable example.

The observant visitor will no doubt notice its small window panes, in the shape of fish scales, which are characteristic of the era in which it was built.

Birmingham Botanical Gardens
Westbourne Road, Edgbaston
Birmingham B15 3TR
Tel.: 0121 454 1860
The gardens cover 15 acres. The Tropical House has a lily pool and lush tropical vegetation. Palms, tree ferns, and orchids are displayed in the Palm House. Outside there is colorful bedding on the Terrace and a tour of the Gardens includes rhododendron walks, a rose garden, a rock garden, and a collection of over 200 trees, as well as charming herb and cottage gardens.

Chatsworth
Bakewell, Baslow
Derbyshire DE45 1PP
Tel.: 01246 565 300
Last surviving element of the famous great greenhouse built by Paxton and Burton between 1836 and 1840. The Duke of Devonshire still casts his shadow over this enchanting park, which measures almost fifty hectares. Home to an orangery dating from 1698, a maze, a herbal garden specializing in medicinal plants, and an arboretum, as well as a fabulous collection of azaleas, rhododendrons, and lupins. The greenhouse, built in 1970, and its range of tropical, Mediterranean, and temperate vegetation are equally worth a look.

The Eden Project
Pentewan, St Austell
Cornwall PL26 6BE,
Tel.: 01726 222 900
Constucted on the site of an old clay quarry, this enormous greenhouse, christened The Eden Project, is in fact the largest greenhouse in the world. Recently inaugurated, it is home to tens of thousands of species from around the globe, which permit the visitor to rediscover the fundamental links between humans and plant life. In years to come, Eden will

undoubtably play a fundamental role in the conservation of plants and the field of biological research.

The Orangery
Kensington Gardens
London SW7
Tel.: 0207 376 0239
If you're visiting London, this is a must. The comforting, tranquil atmosphere beneath the glass roof is conducive to relaxation and daydream.

Royal Botanic Gardens, Kew
Richmond, Surrey
Tel.: 0208 332 5000
Dating back to the same period as the celebrated Crystal Palace, the Kew Palm House's delicate splendor and grace are testimony to the extraordinary ingenuity of Richard Turner, its designer. Boasting a beautiful collection of palm trees, the gardens are a popular destination for Londoners.

Saling Hall
Great Saling, near Braintree, Essex
Comprising six hectares of landscape gardens and an arboretum sheltered by greenery, this splendid greenhouse and its surroundings have a great deal to offer. The greenhouse itself, housing a range of rare species, is a particular delight. One of the finest examples of its type.

Syon Park
Brentford, Middlesex TW8 8JF
Tel.: 0208 560 0883
Designed by the architect Charles Fowler (1791–1867), the Great Conservatory boasts a unique style which lies somewhere between a baroque orangery and a regular greenhouse. Crowned by a remarkable Italian-style dome, its combination of glass and stone achieves striking light effects. The site also houses a wonderful butterfly conservatory.

Tatton Park
Knutsford, Cheshire
WA16 6QN
Tel.: 01625 534 400

www.tattonpark.org.uk

The fernery at Tatton Park bears witness to what was a popular nineteenth-century trend: the importation of exotic plants from distant shores. Built by Paxton in 1850, it plunges the visitor into a world of giants where even adults are dwarfed beneath the towering foliage.

Wales

National Botanic Garden of Wales
Middleton Hall
Llanarthne, Carmarthenshire
Tel.: 01558 668 768
Shaped like a giant transparent carapace, the Great Glasshouse of the Welsh Botanic Garden, created by the architect Sir Norman Foster, was opened to the public in 2000. Measuring 328 feet (100 meters) long and 196 feet (60 meters) wide, it is the largest single-span glasshouse in the world. Its collection of Mediterranean flora is one of the the most beautiful and complete to be found anywhere under one roof. Technical innovations have facilitated the creation of miniature cliffs and waterfalls. The chief goal of this project is to promote public awareness of environmental issues.

Scotland

Botanic Gardens of Glasgow
730 Great Western Road
Glasgow G12 0UE
Tel.: 0141 334 2422/3354
A masterpiece by the eccentric architect John Kibble, Kibble Palace is a splendid illustration of Loudon's theories concerning curvilinear or rounded greenhouses. Miraculously preserved, this ensemble of glasshouses bears moving witness to the era when a sparkling combination of steel and glass was capable of bringing to life the architect's wildest dreams.

Royal Botanic Garden Edinburgh
Inverleith Row
Edinburgh EH3 5LR

Tel.: 0131 552 7171
Dating back to the seventeenth century, Scotland's Royal Botanic Garden now incorporates three very diverse locations for its specialist gardens (see below). As well as being a popular tourist attraction, the gardens are a renowned centre for scientific research and education. The Glasshouse Experience, at the main site, is open all year round and is a must for enthusiasts.
For information on the other sites:
Younger Botanic Garden Benmore
Tel.: 01369 706 261
Logan Botanic garden
Tel.: 01775 860 231
Dawyck Botanic Garden
Tel.: 01721 760 254.

Northern Ireland

The Palm House, Belfast
Botanic Gardens, Stanmills Road Belfast
Tel.: 01232 324 902
Creator of the celebrated Kew gardens, Richard Turner also designed this impressive palm house, which is an excellent example of Victorian architecture.

Republic of Ireland

National Botanic Gardens
Glasnevin, Dublin 8
Tel.: 01 8377 596
Excellently maintained, this botanic garden is home to an attractive variety of plants. The nineteenth-century greenhouses have recently been restored to their original splendor and are a delight to behold.

Canada

Montreal Biodome
4777, avenue Pierre de Coubertin
Montreal, Quebec H1V 1B3
Tel.: 514 868-3000
biodome@ville.montreal.qc.ca
The Biodome, a space-age version of the traditional conservatory complex, was designed to showcase a series of ecosystems typical of the American continents,

from the tropical rainforests of South and Central America to the polar climate of the far North. It is home to a wide range of plant and animal species reflecting this diversity of climatic conditions.

Montreal Botanical Garden
4101 Sherbrooke East, Montreal
Quebec H1X 2B2
Tel.: 514 872-1400
Comprising ten exhibition greenhouses, thirty thematic gardens, and 21,000 species of plant life from the four corners of the globe, this is one of the world's largest and most impressive botanic gardens. The main two-storied exhibition greenhouse, complete with its own waterfall, changes its displays to suit the season.

Royal Botanic Gardens Canada
680 Plains Road West
Burlington, Ontario, L7T 4H4
Tel.: 905 527-1158
The Royal Botanic Gardens claim to offer "fifty different collections to awaken your senses, expand your mind and inspire your own gardening efforts." With the largest lilac collection in the world, two acres of roses, over 100,000 spring bulbs, and an arboretum, this picturesque park is well worth a visit.

France

Auteuil Greenhouses
Av. de la Porte d'Auteuil
75016 Paris
Tel.: 01 46 51 71 20
Designed by Jean-Camille Formigé, these wonderful greenhouses are unparalleled in the French capital. Formerly the municipal supplier to Paris's public parks, their impressive reputation is founded nowadays on the splendid palm house, tropical greenhouse, and the numerous glasshouses which regularly house magnificent exhibitions (azaleas, camellias, fuchsias etc).

Château de Saint-Jean-de-Beauregard
Domaine de Saint-Jean-de-Beauregard

91940 Les Ulis
Tel.: 01 60 12 00 01
In her greenhouses, Muriel de Curel sows seeds and makes cuttings at an incessant pace to prepare flowers which will eventually adorn flower beds and borders. The château plays host to a perennial plant show in the spring and a fruit and vegetable festival in November.

Château de Versailles Orangery
78000 Versailles
Tel.: 01 30 84 74 00
Three thousand fragile trees were once concentrated in this vast gallery which dates back to the era of the Sun King (Louis XIV). The King also had a private collection of fig-trees, over seven hundred of which were brought indoors every winter. Still in use today, the orangery houses over a thousand container plants which include orange trees, pomegranate trees, and numerous rare plants.

Le Jardin des Plantes de Paris
Rue Buffon or Rue Cuvier,
75005 Paris
Originally Louis XIII's medicinal plant garden, the park was opened to the public in the seventeenth century. Showcasing a variety of gardens (Rose, Winter, Alpine) and tropical greenhouses, the botanical garden of Paris contains over 10,000 species. The gardens also house France's Natural History Museum and a small zoo. Entry to the garden is free although there is a small entry fee for the greenhouses, which are open all year round.

Parc de la Tête-d'Or
place Leclerc
69006 Lyon
Tel.: 04 72 82 35 00
Opened to the public in 1857, the park, masterminded by Swiss landscape gardeners Eugène and Denis Bühler, was created to introduce an area of greenery into the city. Since then, it has become home to a botanic garden and an orangery. Its large greenhouses, along with the great dome, were created by the engineer Domenget and are devoted to collections of flora, to breeding plants, and to tropical and aquatic plants, allowing the visitor to observe an impressive diversity of plants.

Phœnix, parc floral de Nice
405, promenade des Anglais
06000 Nice
Tel.: 04 93 18 03 33
The success of Nice's floral park lies in the fact that greenhouses such as these are totally unexpected in Mediterranean climes. Housing a collection of tree ferns and a range of indigenous species, the greenhouses offer a multitude of activities designed to teach young visitors about ecology and botany.

Manufacturers and Suppliers

United States

Amdega/Machin
Westport, CT 06880
Tel.: 800 449 7348
www.amdega.com
American branch of the celebrated 125-year-old British company. Quality hand-crafted designs.

British Conservatories
5004 Mt. Vernon Avenue
Temple, PA 19560
Tel.: 800 566 6360
Designer and fabricator of English style Conservatories available in solid wood and welded aluminum.

Classic Conservatories
1767 RT, 22 West Union
Union, NJ 07083
Tel.: 800-435-1188
Made in Europe, these traditionally styled conservatories and sunrooms can be delivered direct to the customer's home.

Glass House
50, Swedetown Road
Pomfret Center, CT 06259
Tel.: 800-222-3065
From design to installation, Glass House offer a choice of styles, materials, and finishes. Special features include ornamental metalwork as well as variable trims and accessories.

Hartford Conservatories
Woburn, MA 01801
Tel.: 800-963-8700
www.hartford-con.com
Solid mahogany conservatories of traditional English design. Custom designed and modular kits.

Oak Leaf Conservatories
Atlanta, GA 30327
Tel.: 800-360-6283
An English company specializing in custom-built conservatories in America. British designers and craftsmen create, construct, and install conservatories and sunrooms in mahogany and other quality materials.

Private Garden Greenhouse Systems
Hampden, MA 01036
Tel.: 800-287-4769
www.private-garden.com
Another greenhouse company specializing in the construction of English Victorian-style greenhouses and conservatories.

Renaissance Conservatories
132 Ashmore Drive
Leola, PA 17540
Tel.: 800-882-4657
www.renaissance-online.com
Luxury traditional period models as well as a selection of contemporary constructions. Both conservatories and solariums.

Ruby Conservatories
209 East Main Avenue
Zeeland, MI 48040.
Tel.: 616 772 3356
www.rubyconservatories.com
Producing gazebos, sunrooms, greenhouses, orangeries, conservatories in traditional Victorian styles. A winning combination of strong durable materials and charming European style.

Tanglewood Conservatories, Ltd.
Denton, MD 21629
Tel.: 410-479-4700
www.tanglewoodliving.com
Authentic English conservatories, with close attention to detail and stylish embellishment for the authentic touch.

Britain

Amdega Ltd
Faverdale, Darlington,
Co. Durham DL3 OPW,
Tel.: 0800 591 523.
One of the rare Victorian establishments to survive to the present day, Amdega manufacture made-to-measure conservatories in the great English tradition. Made from red cedar-wood with double glazing and doors trimmed with solid copper, these designs are of the utmost luxury and quality.

Appeal Blinds
6, Vale Lane
Bedminster, Bristol BS3 5SD
Tel.: 0800 975 5757
www.appeal-blinds.co.uk
Manufacturers and suppliers of blinds in traditional materials for conservatories.

Arbor Vetum
The Brickyards
Steep Marsh
Petersfield, Hants GU32 2BN
Tel.: 01730 893 000
www.arborvetum.co.uk
This company produces environmentally friendly garden furniture, including benches made from certificated recycled teak.

Finishing Touches
PO Box 65, Norwich NR6 6EJ
Tel.: 0800 585 101
www.finishtouches.com
Specialists in luxury conservatory blinds and furnishings.

Hartley Botanic Ltd
Greenfield, Oldham,
Lancashire
Tel.: 01457 873 244.
Recommended by the celebrated Kew Gardens, this company, founded by Vincent Hartley, offers multi-purpose Victorian greenhouses which combine the skills of times past with the benefits of modern technology. Its prestigious clients, including the Glasgow Botanic Gardens and the Royal Horticultural Society, testify to its impressive reputation.

Machin Conservatories
Faverdale, Darlington
Co Durham
Tel.: 01325 469 100
Recently taken over by Amdega, Machin is now the name of a range by this prestigious company which dates back 120 years. The Machin range offers a series of aluminum models with impeccable finishing which are particularly well suited to large surfaces.

Marston & Langinger
192 Ebury Street, London
Tel.: 0207 823 6829.
Specializing in top-of-the-range constructions, this company, established almost thirty years ago, produces greenhouses destined for locations all over the world. The company's remarkable trademark is the fact that it never reproduces the same model twice. Garden furniture is also available in contemporary designs inspired by models fashionable in the mid-nineteeth century.

Scenic Blue
The Plant Centre
Brogdale Road
Faversham, Kent ME 13 8XZ
Tel.: 01795 533 266
A landscape gardening company that also offers a conservatory accessories service.

Thomas Sanderson
Waterberry Drive
Waterlooville, Hants PO7 7XU
Tel.: 0800 220 603
www.thomas-sanderson.co.uk
Blinds and accessories for the traditional home conservatory.

The Traditional English Conservatory Company Ltd
136, Buckingham Palace Road,
London SW1W 9SA
Tel.: 0207 730 7999
Specializing in conservatories made from treated African mahogany, this company not only creates models for country houses, but also a selection of small verandas for more modest properties. Aimed at making the most of a balcony or a roof, these extensions are also almost entirely soundproof thanks to their incorporation of double-glazed laminated windows.

Vale Garden Houses Ltd.
Melton Road, Harlaxton
Lincolnshire, NG32 1HQ,
Tel.: 01476 564 433
This family-run establishment manufactures conservatories in the Gothic, Victorian, or Edwardian style. From the

smallest to the largest, their conservatories exude all the charm of old England.

Republic of Ireland

Connacht Conservatories
Liosban Estate, Tuam Road, Galway
Tel.: 091 751783
Specialist conservatory company established in 1988. Its expert design service uses a computer-aided design system.

Sunbrite Four Seasons Ltd.
Dublin Road, Julianstown
Co. Meath.
Tel.: 041 982 9129
Design, manufacture, and installation of domestic and commercial conservatories.

Canada

Pacific Sunrooms
3801 NW Fruit Valley Road Ste A
Vancouver WA 98660
Tel.: 888 762-2121
Design and sale of sunrooms and conservatories all over North America.

Tropical Sunrooms Inc.
1486 Victoria St North
Kitchener, Ontario N2B 3E2
Tel.: 519 742-3525
Canada's largest manufacturer of custom sunrooms boasts the only all-glass conservatory, with the most energy-efficient triple glass on the market in North America. Also supplies the United States.

France

Technal
49 rue des Epinettes
75017 Paris
Tel.: 01 46 27 10 20
It is no accident that Technal has become the French leader of the porch and veranda market. Their catalogue features, among others, Victorian-style models, more classical styles, and contemporary designs. The principal material is aluminum.

See also

www.almostimpartialguide.co.uk /conservatories
A handy, easy-to-use consumers' guide to buying a conservatory or orangery, covering a range of aspects from installation to decoration via planning permission, and including a price quotation service.

www.aoc.gov
On this site you will find all the information you need about visiting the U.S. Botanical Gardens in Washington, D.C.

www.conservatoriesonline.com
A site dedicated to providing impartial information on the conservatory and greenhouse market. Includes a list of suppliers in Great Britain, the Republic of Ireland, North America including Canada, and Australia and New Zealand, as well as a discussion forum, advice on planning regulations, and online bookstore.

www.edenproject.com
The official site of the Eden Project in Cornwall—the world's biggest greenhouse and a monumental experiment in how to maintain earth's biodiversity. There is a webcam on site, enabling you to follow developments as they happen.

www.gardenweb.com
A fantastic resource for all those interested in many different aspects of gardening, and including garden listings and discussion forums.

www.greenhousegarden.com
A useful guide to how to make the best of your home greenhouse to cultivate plants and flowers. This site will help you find you local greenhouse gardener's club.

www.greenhouses.uk.net
Conservatory expert Brian Salter provides free advice on purchasing and installing a greenhouse.

www.lloyd-loom.co.uk
Site of Lusty's, UK manufacturers of Lloyd Loom furniture. Includes details on ordering from the United States.

www.lucdhulst.com
Company website of the Belgian-based star greenhouse designer, Luc d'Huslt. Includes pictures of his creations. In English, Dutch and French.

www.nationaltrust.org.uk
The official site of the National Trust, the organization that runs many of Britain's garden attractions, is a mine of useful information and ideas for visits to fabulous gardens and stately homes, many of which have splendid greenhouses and traditional winter gardens.

www.ngs.org.uk
The website of the National Gardens Scheme (see page 128), listing the gardens in Britain open to visitors as part of the scheme over the summer, to raise money for charity.

www.nybg.org/events/agf2001
Details of the annual Antique Garden Furniture Show to be held in the New York Botanical Gardens, featuring specialist antique dealers from across North America.

www.sabot.org/nac/
The site of the San Antonio Botanical Gardens in California, with details of North American conservatories open to the public.

www.ville.montreal.qc.ca/biodome
Visitor's guide to the Montreal Biodome. Includes factsheets on the animals and plants visible on site.

Bibliography

The subject of garden history, greenhouses, and conservatories has long been popular amongst authors. The following publications are highly recommended:

ARCHITECTURE AND HISTORY

Cunningham, Anne. *Crystal Palaces: Garden Conservatories of the United States*. New York: Princeton Architectural Press, 2000.

Hinde, Thomas. *Capability Brown: The Story of a Master Gardener*. New York: Norton, 1986.

Hix, John. *The Glass House*. London: Phaidon, 1974.

Kohlmaier, Georg. *Houses of Glass: a Nineteenth-Century Building Type*. Massachusets, MIT Press, 1991.

Koppelkamm, Stefan. *Glasshouses and Wintergardens of the Nineteenth Century*. Saint Albans: Granada, 1981.

Louis de Malave, Florita. *Greenhouse Architecture: a General Bibliography*. Monticello, Ill.: Vance Bibliographies, 1990.

Repton, Humphry. *An Enquiry into the Changes of Taste in Landscape Gardening*. Farnborough: Gregg, 1969 (first published in 1806).

Stroud, Dorothy. *Humphry Repton*. London: Country Life, 1962.

Woods, May. *Glass Houses: a History of Greenhouses, Orangeries and Conservatories*. New York: Rizzoli, 1988.

GARDENING

Bartok, John. *Greenhouses for Homeowners and Gardeners*. Icatha, NY: NRAES, 2000.

Bonar, Ann. *Complete Guide to Conservatory Plants*. Woodstock, N.Y.: Overlook Press, 1996.

Caplin, Adam, and James Caplin. *Urban Eden*. London: Kyle Cathie, 2000.

Johnson, Hugh. *On Gardening*. London: Mitchell Beazley, 1993.

Mawson, Timothy. *The Garden Room: Bringing Nature Indoors*. New York: Clarkson Potter, 1994.

GREENHOUSE AND CONSERVATORY CONSTRUCTION AND STYLING

Bartholomew, Alexander. *Conservatories and Garden Rooms*. London: Macdonald, 1985.

Curtis, J. *Lloyd Loom: Woven Fibre Furniture*. London: Salamander, 1997.

Freeman, Mark. *Building your own Greenhouse*. Mechanisburg, PA: Stackpole, 1997.

Marston, Peter. *Garden Room Style*. New York: Rizzoli, 1998.

The Book of the Conservatory. London: Weidenfeld and Nicolson, 1992.

Tressider, Jane and Stafford Cliff. *Living under Glass*. London: Thames and Hudson, 1986.

Trust Dahan, Bonnie. *Gardenhouse: Bringing the Outside In*. San Francisco: Chronicle Books, 1999.

VISITS

Lacey, Stephen. *Gardens of the National Trust*. London: National Trust, 1992.

Rothschild, Miriam. *The Rothschild Gardens*. London: Gala, 1996.

Wyman, Donald. *Arboretums and Botanical Gardens of North America*. Jamaica Plain, Mass.: Harvard University, 1959.

Photographic Credits

Index

Acknowledgments

The editor of this work wishes to extend very warm thanks to the green-house and conservatory manufacturers and suppliers who were kind enough to provide answers to a number of questions on the subject, which were most valuable. Particular thanks are due to the following companies, who permitted the editor and author to access their archives and sales material: Amdega, Luc d'Hulst, Marston and Langinger, Serres et Ferronneries d'Antan, Vale Garden Houses. We also wish to thank the private individuals and institutions who so generously allowed us to visit their wonderful greenhouses and conservatories. Without their valuable aid, this work would not have been possible.

Translated from the French by Lisa Davidson
Additional research by Jodie Rees
Copy-editing: Sandra Raphael
Color separation: Sele Offset
Design: Marc Walter / Chine
Typesetting: Studio X-Act, Paris

Originally published as *Serres et Jardins d'Hiver*
© 2000 Flammarion
English-language edition
© 2001 Flammarion

ISBN 2-08010-585-X
FA0585-01-VI
Dépôt légal: 09/2001

Printed in France by Pollina s.a., 85400 Luçon - n° L83745